Which Way's Up?

Which Way's Up?

The future for coalition Britain and how to get there

Nick Boles

First published in Great Britain in 2010 by
Biteback Publishing Ltd
Heal House
375 Kennington Lane
London
SE11 5QY

ISBN 978-1-84954-063-6

10 9 8 7 6 5 4 3 2 1

A CIP catalogue record for this book is available from the British Library.

Set in Minion and Frutiger
Printed and bound in Great Britain by CPI Cox and Wyman, Reading, RG1 8EX

For my parents, all three of them

Contents

Acknowledgements

I would like to thank Theodore Agnew, Dudley Fishburn, Phil Hulme, Edmund Lazarus, Laurie Magnus, John Nash, Lisbet Rausing, George Robinson, Richard Sharp and Dennis Stevenson for their generous sponsorship of this project. Their backing does not imply that they share my views or support either the Conservative Party or the Coalition. I am also grateful to Janan Ganesh, Michael Lynas and Ben Moxham for their help with some of the ideas and arguments that follow. Responsibility for any errors and stupidities is mine alone.

Introduction

Britain's new Prime Minister arrived in Downing Street on the evening of 11 May 2010 and paid generous tribute to the outgoing Labour government, noting that 'compared with a decade ago, this country is more open at home and more compassionate abroad.' He was right to do so. Labour can be justly proud of the legislation that has given full equality to gay people, strengthened the place of women in society and delivered much greater respect for, and inclusion of, people from ethnic minority backgrounds. They can also celebrate the progress they made in increasing Britain's aid to the developing world and the leadership they showed in the fight against global poverty. But David Cameron's carefully chosen words skated around a harsher truth: that, in most respects, the last ten years have been, for Britain, a wasted decade.

The wasted decade

In 1997, Labour had an extraordinary opportunity: the economy was growing steadily, Tony Blair had won a huge majority in Parliament and the public finances were in an enviable state. This was the moment to act boldly. Labour should have promised the public sector real growth in spending in exchange for radical reform to bring in competition among those who provide public services and choice for members of the public. They should have said to public sector workers: we will give you better pay, increase the number of frontline workers and invest in modern, high-quality facilities, if you accept changes to working practices that will increase your productivity. Instead, Labour wasted their first term, scrapping the internal market reforms in the NHS and grant-maintained schools in education, and sticking to Conservative spending plans until the public began to protest. Then they opened the floodgates and unleashed a tidal wave of cash that pushed up costs, paid for some good new buildings and equipment, but washed over the inherited central planning structures of the NHS and state education, leaving their fundamental flaws intact.

The same sad tale of missed opportunities characterises Labour's record on welfare reform and employment. A buoyant economy and full Treasury coffers provided the perfect platform for radical reforms to confront the culture of permanent worklessness, which imprisons millions of men and women in soul-destroying subsistence on meagre benefits. Never again will circumstances be so benign. This was the moment to experiment with hiring independent contractors to get people back to work and paying them according to their success in doing so. This was the time when a Labour government, with its proud belief in the moral worth of work, could have introduced compulsory community work programmes, to ensure that able-bodied adults claiming benefits for more than a year or two would have to work for their dole money. Instead, having pledged to 'think the unthinkable', Labour threw their one true reformer, Frank Field, overboard and sat back, while hundreds of thousands of migrant workers came into the country to take the low-paid jobs that British citizens had no reason or motivation to accept.

The same unwillingness to take difficult decisions to secure long-term benefit characterised Labour's approach to the old problem of energy security and the new challenge of climate change. It has been obvious for a long time that Britain's existing nuclear power stations will have to be taken out of production over the next few years, that the process of securing planning consent and then building new nuclear capacity will not be quick, that our increasing reliance on imported gas, while helpful in cutting carbon emissions relative to oil and coal, is making Britain dangerously dependent on unstable and potentially unfriendly regimes, and that it will take a sustained commitment over several decades for renewable energy sources to supply a significant proportion of the country's energy needs. All of these facts were known to ministers, so there is really no excuse for Labour's failure to build more gas storage, create a simple and consistent scheme to subsidise investment in renewables, invest in grid improvements to cater for renewable production in Scotland and the North Sea, and start the process of commissioning new nuclear reactors so that they come on stream before the existing capacity is shut down. The fact that they did none of these things means that Britain faces the possibility of power cuts for the first time in forty years and has very little chance of meeting the target of supplying 20 per cent of our energy from renewable sources by 2020.

The fundamental flaw at the heart of the New Labour project was this. Having spent fifteen years developing bold plans to recast Britain but neglecting to do what was necessary to win an election, the Labour Party was taken over by a small elite of ruthless pragmatists, whose single-minded obsession was to win the next election, to win big, and, once they had done so, to start work on winning the one after that. They had no analysis of the big challenges facing the country, no theory to explain how things could be transformed for the better, and no grander mission than to be the first Labour government to win and complete a second term in office. They realised this goal, and handsomely surpassed it. But, in their fixation with electoral success, they passed up the opportunity to grapple with big problems and implement big changes. And so a decade went to waste.

The coalition

In May 2010, at the end of a long and deep recession, with government borrowing at an all-time record and British troops being killed every week in Afghanistan, a new government was formed. Not just a new government but a new kind of government, taking Britain on a journey that none of us has been on before. Unconvinced by each of the parties on offer, and certain only that they despised the political system that had governed Britain for the last sixty years, the voters stumbled their way towards an outcome, which has forced that system into sudden, radical change. As a result, we have a Liberal Democrat–Conservative coalition government that secured the support of 60 per cent of the voters, that has a comfortable majority in the House of Commons and that draws on talents as formidable and diverse as those of Vince Cable and Iain Duncan Smith.

The negotiation of the coalition government's programme took remarkably little time and, while some contentious issues had to be parked in the policy limbo of the independent review, a number of bold reforms remained intact, not least the liberalisation of state schools, radical welfare reform and a whole slew of constitutional changes such as the introduction of an elected upper chamber and a referendum on the introduction of the Alternative Vote for future general elections. Enacting and then implementing these reforms will certainly keep the government busy for the first year or two. But the coalition will need to go further and be bolder if it is to steer Britain out of the doldrums in which it became becalmed at the end of the wasted decade.

It implies no criticism of either party's leadership to observe that the coalition agreement is a blend of two manifestos and, in some places, has had to settle for the lowest common denominator between them. As election manifestos are themselves compromises, artfully constructed to display radicalism without doing anything to spook the horses, to woo floating voters without doing anything to drive away long-standing supporters, it is inevitable that they fall short as long-term programmes for government. This book is my attempt to do what no-one has yet done and look beyond the next two years to outline a radical programme for a two-term Liberal Democrat–Conservative coalition government.

Why me?

I have spent nearly ten years campaigning for the Conservative Party to become more liberal. In 2001, I published *A Blue Tomorrow: New Visions for Modern Conservatives* with Michael Gove and Ed Vaizey, which argued for a Conservatism 'which is more sensitive to the changing social mores of Britain' and asserted that 'the Tories must become capable of speaking to all the British people in an appealing tone and proving constructive about the future.' In 2002, I set up Policy Exchange with Michael Gove and Francis Maude to be the forum and idea factory for a modern, liberal centre right. It was at Policy Exchange that James O'Shaughnessy, now director of policy at 10 Downing Street, first coined the phrase 'progressive ends through conservative means'. It was also at Policy Exchange that, in 2005, we developed the blueprints for Gove's education reforms and, in particular, for the idea of a 'pupil premium', which was adopted by both the Conservatives and Liberal Democrats and is now a key plank of the coalition programme. I am genuinely delighted that the Conservatives have gone into government in coalition with Liberal Democrats and hope that, in one form or another, Britain will have a government that combines the best bits of liberalism with the best bits of conservatism for the rest of this decade.

But the coalition government will need strong, forward momentum if it is to survive the inevitable arguments and reversals that it will encounter. The best way to achieve this momentum is to identify the fundamental values and beliefs that most Conservatives and Liberal Democrats share and ensure that the government has a busy programme of action that will deliver them. A common commitment to promoting shared beliefs will provide a gravitational force to stop the coalition flying apart.

Where Gladstone and Thatcher meet

It should not surprise anyone to find a great deal of common ground between Liberal Democrats and modern Conservatives. Margaret Thatcher herself once said, 'I would not mind betting that if Mr Gladstone were alive today he would apply to join the Conservative Party.' It is certainly the case that, in her impatience with inherited privilege, Mrs Thatcher drew more from classical nineteenth-century liberalism than the Tory tradition. Modern Conservatism is itself a cocktail that contains liberal flavours. Both Conservatives and Liberal Democrats are inspired by the example of great civic leaders such as Joseph Chamberlain, who led the Liberal Unionists into a coalition with the Conservative Party. The greatest Prime Minister the Conservative Party has ever produced, Winston Churchill, was a Liberal MP for twenty years from 1904, and only left the Conservative Party because it had turned its back on the principle of free trade, a principle that both parties now share.

If the coalition is a big top pitched on ground that is common to modern Conservatives and Liberal Democrats, its blue and yellow striped canvas is held up by five sturdy posts, each of which is planted in the solid earth of shared principles, values and beliefs. The first, and most important, piece of common ground is the paramount importance that we both attach to personal freedom and the right of every individual to live their life in the way they choose, subject only to constraints on their freedom to act in a way that harms others. This shared focus on the freedom of the individual leads both Conservatives and Liberal Democrats to feel genuine horror at the overweening power of central government and its treatment of citizens either as supplicants, dependent on the generosity of the state for income and public services, or as lab rats in some vast social experiment, designed to improve mankind.

The second piece of common ground is a belief that the mission of a progressive government, like this coalition, should be to offer more opportunities to those who have been born in poverty or inherited other disadvantages, and to help them convert these opportunities into real improvements in their lives. Our commitment to personal freedom, and our shared suspicion of socialist utopias, mean that we will never be duped by the left's claims that government action can make people equal. But we are impatient for a government that focuses money and attention on helping people pull themselves up out of deprivation, and we do not accept that it is right for Britain to be divided into one country for the rich and another for the poor.

The third piece of common ground is our sense of responsibility for the natural world and the health of our planet. Neither party believes that money makes the world go around; neither is willing to accept that the price of prosperity is a gradual poisoning of our planet's oceans, forests and skies. But, in designing policies to combat climate change, we share an innate scepticism about fine phrases and grand plans. What we want from our coalition is a relentless focus on the practical steps that will give people and businesses and communities both the power and the incentive to cut carbon dioxide emissions in their daily lives.

The fourth point of common ground is our shared understanding that Britain's prosperity is not guaranteed, that every generation must earn its way in the world, and that we will be condemning our children and grandchildren to a grim future of decline, if we duck our current fiscal problems, postpone the day when public sector profligacy is reined in or delude ourselves that the mirage of easy money that disfigured the last decade can be conjured up again.

The fifth piece of common ground is our belief that local communities should be given the power and freedom to take charge of their own destinies, and that, to do so, they need strong and independent local government, representing the wishes of local people and trying out new ways of doing things that will make life better for them.

This book is a result of the application of these shared values and beliefs to the biggest challenges facing Britain in 2010. I have tried to avoid a shopping list of issues and policies, and instead have sought to tell a story about the way the coalition government should think about each of the big challenges and the principles that should guide the development of policy.

So Chapter 1 addresses the question of where Britain's future prosperity is going to come from and rejects the ideological posturing of both the Luddite left and the ultra-free-market right in favour of hard-nosed pragmatism and a realistic assessment of Britain's competitive advantages. Chapter 2 links the recent political crisis as a result of the MPs' expenses scandal to Liberal Democrat and Conservative objections to the power of the central state and argues for a rapid acceleration in the transfer of power and responsibility, both from central government departments to local authorities, and from all forms of bureaucracy to individuals, households and communities.

Some commentators have warned that the fiscal crisis will make it impossible for the government to make radical changes in the way that it makes decisions and delivers services to members of the public. I disagree. Chapter 3 shows how the unavoidable pressure to make drastic cuts in public expenditure can drive a set of far-reaching reforms to free up our public services – and argues that it is only by giving choice to the people using public services, creating competition among the institutions that provide them, and fostering local experimentation and innovation, not just inside government but out in communities, that we have any chance of achieving dramatic savings without forfeiting the values we cherish.

Chapter 4 addresses the divisions between rich and poor, those in work and those living on benefits, and challenges the view that income inequality is the main cause of Britain's social problems, arguing that it is through emancipation of our schools and liberalisation of social housing, as well as through new programmes like National Citizen Service for young people, that we will recreate the glue that binds people together and restore trust to our society. Chapter 5 confronts the challenge of excessive immigration, from both inside and outside the European Union, and proposes some bold but practical measures to build a sense of solidarity between people born here and people who move here so that Britain remains one, unified, nation.

Chapter 6 makes the case for brutal honesty about our dependence on imported fossil fuels and suggests that it will require hard-headed calculation to ensure that we avoid power cuts towards the end of this decade while bringing about a long-term shift to a low-carbon way of life. Finally, in Chapter 7, I chart a new global landscape of opportunities and risks as the solitary dominance of the American superpower wanes and new giants in Asia and Latin America are roused from their slumbers, and I propose a foreign policy of 'British Gaullism', which uses all our resources, including our growing aid budget, to promote British interests around the world.

There are some ideas in this book that will make some of my Conservative colleagues uneasy. There will be others that the more left-leaning Liberal Democrats will find hard to swallow. Taken together, I hope that they achieve a synthesis that is both true to the fundamental values which bind our two parties and equal to the huge challenges facing our country.

At the end of Labour's wasted decade, Britain is socially divided, lacks economic confidence and harbours doubts about its destiny. The coalition government has an opportunity born out of crisis. Nobody disputes that dramatic changes are needed to revive our economy, renew the bonds of community or restore our sense of national purpose. We cannot afford to waste another ten years. We need a decade of bold reform and purposeful leadership to make Britain envied the world over for its economic dynamism, social harmony and international clout.

1. Why prosperity matters and
how to get it back

Developments during the last decade have given lots of ammunition to enemies of capitalism. It has become clear that man's activities are contributing to a dramatic increase in greenhouse gases in the upper atmosphere and that this will bring about a significant rise in global temperatures, if left unchecked. There has been growing evidence that increases in wealth beyond the level required to satisfy basic material needs of clothing, shelter and food do not produce equivalent increases in happiness. And the decade ended with a devastating financial crisis, caused by the reckless greed of the people running the power supply of capitalism.

Against such a backdrop, it is surprising that the anti-capitalist left haven't swept all before them in elections around the world. But the fact that they have not found a way to translate the events of the last ten years into support for an alternative approach does not absolve politicians on the centre-right of the obligation to answer two serious questions about capitalism. The first asks whether it is right for advanced societies like ours to make increases in prosperity a prime objective of government policy. The second asks whether free markets are still the best way to organise the allocation of resources to satisfy human wants and needs. Only when we have answered these two questions will we have laid the foundations for a new economic policy, one that recognises recent failures and excesses and is designed to ensure that they are not repeated.

Economic growth – is it worth it?

In the twentieth century, both capitalists and socialists shared the presumption that increased prosperity, or, to use the technical term, economic growth, should be a central goal of government policy. Their arguments focused on how the benefits of this growth should be distributed and on how decisions about the allocation of resources to different economic activities should be made. Now, for the first time since the industrial revolution, mainstream thinkers and writers are questioning this presumption, and are asking whether economic growth makes people happier.

The debate begins with the suggestion that gross national product is a flawed measure of progress, because it fails to capture many of the things that people really value. Robert Kennedy put it best:

> The gross national product includes air pollution and advertising for cigarettes, and ambulances to clear our highways of carnage. It counts special locks for our doors, and jails for the people who break them. GNP includes the destruction of the redwoods and the death of Lake Superior. It grows with the production of napalm and missiles and nuclear warheads . . . And if GNP includes all this, there is much that it does not comprehend. It does not allow for the health of our families, the quality of their education, or the

joy of their play. It is indifferent to the decency of our factories and the safety of our streets alike. It does not include the beauty of our poetry or the strength of our marriages, or the intelligence of our public debate or the integrity of our public officials ... GNP measures neither our wit nor our courage, neither our wisdom nor our learning, neither our compassion nor our devotion to our country. It measures everything, in short, except that which makes life worthwhile.

In 2009, at the invitation of President Sarkozy, two Nobel Prize-winning economists, Joseph Stiglitz and Amartya Sen, delivered a somewhat more prosaic rehearsal of the same arguments, stressing the failures of accounting measures like GDP to capture the effects of pollution, and urging political leaders to aim for broader measures of social progress, like the availability of healthcare and education. Some modern critics of economic growth go further than this. The champions of '*décroissance*' – which can be crudely translated as 'de-growth' – do not just argue that there is more to life than money. They suggest that the process of striving after more money is reducing human welfare and that we should actively seek a lower level of material production and consumption, which is environmentally sustainable and more fairly distributed.

Supporters of the new government need to take these arguments seriously, because the credibility of our economic system has been seriously weakened by the financial crisis and the recession that has followed. But taking them seriously should not mean capitulation. We should start by acknowledging that Kennedy was right: we have always valued much more than just money. Freedom, independence, the security of our country and the strength of our families and communities: these are all values for which Liberal Democrats and Conservatives have been willing to make economic sacrifices. It was the Communists who elevated material accumulation above all other goals – Stalin's slaughter of the kulaks through collectivisation and the poisoning of Lake Baikal provided eloquent evidence of the far left's willingness to subordinate life, freedom and the natural world to the relentless drive for economic power. But, while it is obvious that we should pursue broader social objectives and not elevate the false god of GDP growth above all others, we must also insist that none of our broader social goals will be achievable unless we can restore economic growth – and sustain it in the future.

In the years of plenty that characterised most of the last decade, it was easy to criticise the shallow materialism of fashion-conscious, brand-obsessed shoppers. It came as no surprise to find that rampant consumerism fuelled by cheap credit was not necessarily making anyone happier. But, after two years of deep recession, we now see that the greatest victims of declining prosperity are those with least to start with. If the freelance consultant husband of a successful City lawyer finds his work drying up, the quality of his family's life may improve, as he is suddenly able to take the kids to school, to cook them their tea and help them with their homework. But, if the Asda checkout lady married to a lorry driver has her hours cut, this does not herald a welcome recalibration of their work–life balance. It causes stress, suffering and a squeezing of opportunities for their children. There's less money for books and school trips – and her husband has to take on more weekend jobs to the continent, missing his son's football matches and Saturday nights spent watching *The X Factor* with the whole family.

Economic retrenchment also hits government's support for the public goods that Stiglitz and Sen would put at the heart of a true measurement of progress. A Chancellor who receives growing revenues from corporation tax and income tax as the economic pie gets bigger can invest in new equipment and better facilities, pay nurses and teachers more, and give every neighbourhood its own police officer. A Chancellor who confronts a collapse in tax revenues at the end of a long recession has to make painful cuts in public spending, reduce the number of students able to go to university, and may be forced to slash grants to museums and theatres and block the offer of expensive new drugs to all who might benefit from them.

Economic growth does not guarantee progress or happiness or personal fulfilment. But the absence of growth makes these things a lot harder to come by. Restoring economic growth should not be the only goal of the coalition government. It isn't even the most important. But it must be its most urgent priority – because, without growth, the poorest suffer most and social progress becomes impossible.

Free markets RIP?

The next question, then, is how to deliver the economic growth we need. Until the collapse of Lehman Brothers, it was generally accepted that free markets provided the most efficient way of allocating resources to different economic activities. But firms like Lehman operated in the ultimate free market and ended up destroying themselves, nearly taking the whole capitalist system down with them. The licence given to such institutions to innovate, speculate and reward their employees rested on the firm belief that they would be rational in their pursuit of greater prosperity for their shareholders – and that they would not therefore take disproportionate risks. As former Federal Reserve chairman Alan Greenspan put it, in his evidence to the United States Senate:

> I made a mistake in presuming that the self-interest of organisations, specifically banks, is such that they were best capable of protecting shareholders and equity in the firms . . . I discovered a flaw in the model that I perceived is the critical functioning structure that defines how the world works. I had been going for forty years with considerable evidence that it was working exceptionally well.

Confronted by the reality that tens of thousands of free agents, backed by sophisticated systems to measure risk, nevertheless ran lemming-like off a precipice and into the abyss, we have to ask ourselves whether we shouldn't abandon free markets and develop a much more strongly guided approach to economic development. That banks need much tighter regulation is a given – the existence of government guarantees for bank deposits and the role of the banks in providing the fuel on which the entire economic system depends make this essential. The key question is whether we shouldn't also modify our approach to economic development in general. In searching for the sources of new economic growth, should the new government stick to the traditional free market cocktail of deregulation and tax cuts? Or should it develop new forms of intervention, to stimulate investment and build on Britain's competitive advantages?

We should start by recognising that free markets are neither God given nor the inevitable product of evolution. They are institutions, created by man, and based on a wide range of artificial interventions in the natural way of doing things: property rights, contract law and restraints on monopolies and price-fixing, to name a few. Their particular advantage is that, once created, they empower vast numbers of individuals to use their own intelligence and ingenuity to seek advantage by offering an improvement in something that someone else values. But, because even large groups of people can be affected by mood swings, it is quite possible for free markets to get things wrong, to underestimate risk and to set prices that do not reflect underlying reality. And there are some areas where free markets consistently produce socially and economically inferior outcomes – which is why most advanced economies have given government responsibility for guaranteeing the provision of schools, roads and policing. Even under Thatcher and Reagan, free markets were never as unbridled or as ubiquitous as either their supporters or opponents liked to pretend.

We should also recognise that the rising economic powers, whose growth will dominate the next few decades, are highly selective in their commitment to the free market. Nobody who has been to a Guangzhou trade fair can be in any doubt that the free market operates with savage efficiency in Communist China. But the Chinese government is autocratic in its control of the country's economic strategy and investment priorities. Reliant as we are on international trade, Britain does not have the luxury of standing back and allowing the free market to determine how our economy develops, for the prospects of British businesses are hugely influenced by the strongly interventionist exchange rate and industrial policies of countries that are both major competitors and vast markets.

Economic strategy

This new economic order requires a new economic strategy. The coalition government should take a leaf out of Michael Heseltine's book in its approach to Britain's economic development and combine ruthless pragmatism with total dedication to promoting the national interest. We should be unsentimental in our calculations as to where Britain's competitive advantages lie – and should not be overly fastidious about the methods we employ to ensure that we establish a global lead in the relevant sectors. We should not apologise for interventions to improve the country's economic competitiveness. Nor should we shrink from aggressive tactics in international negotiations, to secure opportunities for British business.

In developing a new economic strategy, we must first identify the likely sources of future economic growth. If Britain is to return to healthy levels of GDP growth, it cannot be on the basis of a boom in domestic consumption, whether public or private. Households still face very high levels of indebtedness, much of it underpinned by property whose value is precarious. With interest rates likely to return to normal levels as the Bank of England unwinds quantitative easing, there is little prospect of private consumers resuming the credit-fuelled spending spree that characterised the Noughties, and it would be undesirable for them to do so. The government will also have to cut its consumption in order to cut the deficit. So the only way that Britain will be able to restore economic growth is through a strong revival in investment and exports.

Investment

The most important factor in determining investment activity is the level of long-term interest rates. The government is right to make deficit reduction its overriding objective, because sustained government borrowing at current levels would cause long-term rates to rise and would choke off the tentative recovery in business investment. I look at how deficit reduction should be approached in Chapter 3.

According to the Office for Budget Responsibility, business investment fell nearly 20 per cent in 2009 as a result of the credit crunch. As the banks repair their balance sheets and credit begins to become available again, investment should rebound, so long as interest rates remain low. The OBR has forecast total fixed investment growth of just under 4 per cent in 2011 and just under 8 per cent in 2012. But we should not sit back and wait for low interest rates and growing global demand to float the British economy off the rocks. The new government needs to implement active policies to stimulate investment and boost demand for British goods and services.

As a first step, the government must maintain its own investment in the country's competitive base, even as it cuts back on overall levels of public expenditure. The coalition has decided to maintain the public investment plans set out by the last government, which would see public net investment fall from £49 billion (3.4 per cent of GDP) in 2009/10 to £39 billion (2.8 per cent of GDP) in 2010/11, £27 billion (or 1.8 per cent of GDP) in 2011/12, £24 billion (1.6 per cent of GDP) in 2012/13 and £20 billion (1.2 per cent of GDP) in 2013/14. There is certainly scope to rein back investment in building new schools and hospitals and no need to repeat the emergency investments that were brought forward to support economic activity during the recession, but I hope that the Chancellor will find room to boost public investment levels in 2012/13 and 2013/14. We need to continue investment in vital economic infrastructure if we are to stimulate sustained growth in private sector investment and export demand. In particular, we should press on with the construction of Crossrail in London and accelerate investment in the construction of high-speed railways linking London with Birmingham, Manchester and Glasgow.

While continued public investment in economic infrastructure is vital, it is private investment that will be the key to recovery. The centrepiece of the government's policies to support business investment is the bold plan for cuts in corporation tax, set out by George Osborne in the emergency Budget. Businesses now have a strong incentive to make investments in the next couple of years, because the profits that these investments generate thereafter will be subject to some of the lowest rates of taxation in the OECD.

Export promotion

Exports will be the other main source of economic growth in the next few years. The devaluation of sterling has certainly created the conditions for export growth and every British family should thank Heaven (and Gordon Brown) that we never joined the euro. But export volumes have been slow to respond. As Martin Wolf of the *Financial Times* has pointed out, export demand needs to come from somewhere else on planet Earth. We cannot all run trade surpluses with Mars. So, if exports are to drive economic growth, we need to see a rapid increase in demand from China and the other countries that have been running persistent trade surpluses. Currently, there is little sign of the necessary shift in either government policy or consumer attitudes in the surplus countries.

The coalition should take an aggressive approach towards export promotion. Working in concert with the United States and those other countries whose consumer booms and persistent deficits supported global economic growth in the Noughties, the Prime Minister and Chancellor should put significant and sustained pressure on China, Germany and the other surplus countries to rebalance their economies and boost domestic consumption, so that the markets for British exports expand. The government should appoint a well-known figure with outstanding international contacts to lead the campaign to win major contracts for British companies. Although it will stick in the craw of many Conservatives, Lord Mandelson would be the best candidate. The contacts and experience he acquired in his years as Secretary of State for Trade and Industry, European trade commissioner and then Business Secretary give him unique qualifications to be the country's chief salesman. We should put party differences and personality clashes to one side, and give Mandy a new mandate: to do whatever it takes to win business for Britain. If sealing the deal means giving him yet another new title, I am sure Vince Cable won't mind giving up the right to call himself President of the Board of Trade.

In his campaign to expand British exports, Mandelson should be able to call on all of the country's finest assets: leading museums and galleries, our best theatre companies and orchestras, even the Royal Family. They all receive public subsidy and should all be expected to do their bit to help promote Britain abroad. The 2012 Olympics offers a particular opportunity. We should use it to bring major potential customers (and investors) to Britain, to give them VIP treatment at the Games (which have, after all, cost the British taxpayer and lottery player over £9 billion) and to showcase the best that Britain has to offer. The Prime Minister and the Chancellor should host dinners in Downing Street and Somerset House. The Queen should be asked to hold receptions at Buckingham Palace and Windsor Castle. Leading sporting stars such as David Beckham and Lewis Hamilton should be persuaded to fly the flag in front of the biggest buyers from around the world. For three weeks, Britain will be in the spotlight, watched by the whole world. We must seize this moment to help Britain's exporters go for gold, not just our athletes.

Industrial strategy

If we are to maximise Britain's economic potential, we need an industrial strategy too. The coalition must identify the sectors where Britain has the chance to become a global leader, and devote real effort to helping them compete. Purists may argue against what they will call 'picking winners'. But our international competitors are pitiless in their determination to dominate the key industries of the future. We need to climb down from the pulpit of free market theory and start hustling in the global marketplace if we want British businesses to succeed. Some of this help might be financial, although the budget deficit means that there will be precious little cash to spare for old-fashioned subsidies. Most of it will involve using all the influence and clout of government to open doors, clear away obstacles and stop other bits of government policy from getting in the way.

Britain's industrial strategy should be rooted in a clear understanding of the forces that will shape economic developments around the world in the next twenty years and an unsentimental analysis of the opportunities and risks that they present a country of Britain's size, location, skills, and other attributes. Two of the most important forces will be the rising prosperity of China, India and Brazil and the global move towards a low-carbon way of life.

The new middle classes of Asia and Latin America

It is conventional to talk of the competitive threat posed by China, India and Brazil. Having spent nearly ten years of my life running a small manufacturing business that made paint brushes and rollers, and having seen its profitability destroyed by the low-cost and ever-improving quality of imports from China, I am all too aware of the ways in which Britain might lose out to a vast new workforce of people who are well educated and work harder for less. And the threat is not confined to low-tech manufacturing. Design, engineering, research, software development: these are all activities which, increasingly, can be outsourced from highly qualified graduates in Shanghai or Bangalore.

But the growing prosperity and education of tens of millions of Chinese, Indians and Brazilians will create opportunities for British businesses too. When people join the middle class, their horizons expand. They want to learn English, to send their children to study at great universities and colleges, to travel to the world's most famous and historic places, to buy leading brands and own examples of iconic design, to watch films, read books and listen to music from the English-speaking world. They also want to save money for their retirement, to make investments and to acquire properties abroad. Britain is well placed to capitalise on this massive increase in demand for aspirational goods and services. There are three areas in particular where government has a crucial role to play in ensuring that Britain benefits from the rise of a global middle class: education, entertainment and financial services.

The first step for any foreign student who hasn't grown up in an English-speaking society is to learn English. Once someone has made the effort to travel to the UK to learn English, they are much more likely to return to study at university or business school, as well as to form relationships and develop an affection for Britain that will make them a long-term customer, investor, visitor and ally. So the coalition must rein in the overzealous officials in the UK Border Agency, who are making it impossible for young people with a genuine desire to learn English to get a student visa. While there is no doubt that an excessively lax regime allowed tens of thousands of people, who had no intention of studying in the UK, to enrol at bogus colleges, the panic measures taken by the last government in response to growing public anger over the abuse of our immigration system threaten grave damage not just to Britain's English-language schools but to our future economic prosperity. The coalition should make the visa application process for legitimate students as simple and straightforward as possible, while focusing its resources on tough enforcement action to drive out cowboy colleges and deport the economic migrants who have exploited the student visa system to get into the country just to work.

If English-language schools form an important gateway

through which foreign students first come to Britain, it is our universities and colleges that provide the strongest magnet for the children of the new middle classes in Asia and Latin America to form a relationship with this country. A degree from a British university has a cachet that will become more valuable, not less, as ambitious youngsters and their pushy parents seek to differentiate themselves from the millions studying at home. It is inevitable that public funding to subsidise places for British students will be cut, so it is all the more important that the government does whatever is necessary to support the efforts of universities and colleges to attract more foreign students. It should encourage the establishment of more private universities like BPP and free existing public universities to become more commercial in the development of the courses they offer and the marketing of them around the world. In particular, we must not allow those charged with the difficult task of stopping would-be terrorists from getting into the country to resort to crude limits on the number of visas for students from Muslim countries such as Malaysia. Government action to deter illegal immigration and prevent infiltration by terrorists must be more like a laser and less like a blunderbuss, if we are to make Britain the place that India's best software developers, China's best engineers and Brazil's best bioethanol producers acquire their qualifications and first taste the freedom of living away from home.

Entertainment is another area in which opportunities for Britain will expand dramatically as the world gets wealthier. The new middle classes will want to read the 2020 equivalents of *Harry Potter* and *The Da Vinci Code*, buy tickets for that decade's *Les Mis* or *Phantom of the Opera*, listen to the next Coldplay or Kylie, and go to the cinema to see the next James Bond. If

British writers, editors, sound engineers, actors, make-up artists, animators, drummers and photographers are to benefit from this surge in global demand for our creative output, the government needs to make international enforcement of copyright laws a key objective of our foreign policy. In the early eighteenth century, the British navy hunted down pirates to keep the sea lanes clear for British trade with India, South America and the Far East. In the twenty-first century, the British government needs to be equally aggressive in its prosecution of the cyber-pirates. The survival of every business that publishes creative content is at stake and no country has more to lose from failure in this battle than ours.

The new middle classes live in countries which offer little or nothing in the way of state pensions. They will want to accumulate assets, both to pay for a comfortable old age and to pass on to their children and grandchildren. Being the world's most open and international financial centre, the City of London is in pole position to provide investment opportunities for this new generation of capitalists. While it is right for the government to introduce a bank levy and to insist on much tighter regulation of the banks, whose lax management and reckless greed cost taxpayers tens of billions of pounds, we must resist any measures that might undermine the fund managers, insurance companies, private equity firms and hedge funds, who played little part in the financial crisis and who are poised to attract the savings of new global middle class. The EU hedge fund directive is a good example. If our European partners do not listen to the British government's arguments, we should follow the French or Italian example – and refuse to implement any regulations that would damage our national interest.

Low-carbon living

As well as focusing on the opportunities created by the new middle classes of Asia and Latin America, Britain's industrial strategy should also focus on the opportunities resulting from global efforts to take the carbon out of capitalism. Ministers should not waste their time or taxpayers' money on trying to catch up with the Chinese manufacturers of solar panels or Brazilian producers of bioethanol. Instead they should focus on areas where Britain has innate advantages, such as offshore energy resources, and inherited skills, such as those developed by the offshore oil and gas industry. Shortly after the election, the National Grid announced that it is planning to invest £22 billion in the UK grid over the next five years and confirmed that much of this will go on offshore transmission networks and the creation of a smart grid. This is just the kind of infrastructure that Britain needs to unlock growth in low-carbon businesses and jobs.

Don't forget the supply side

While an industrial strategy can help channel scarce resources into sectors which might make a big difference to the country's prosperity, the best entrepreneurs and managers cannot make bricks without straw. In the long run, nothing will be more important to Britain's future competitiveness than the skills of the British people. This is why there is no more important reform in the new government's programme than the liberation of schools from stifling bureaucratic control and the creation of a pupil premium to channel extra resources to the schooling of young people from deprived backgrounds. I discuss how we might entrench and extend these reforms in Chapter 4.

We also need to improve our record in nurturing and developing people who can create, innovate and manage. To do this, we need to allow our universities to increase tuition fees and develop alternative sources of income. We should encourage them to be shamelessly elitist, on condition that their elitism is intellectual, not financial: they should offer places to the best students, regardless of their means, and then use government funding and charitable endowments to finance loans and grants so that every student who is offered a place can afford to take it up.

If we are going to set universities free from bureaucratic control, we also need to put in place incentives for them to deliver economic benefits to Britain. While the pursuit of knowledge for its own sake is an admirable endeavour, Britain's current plight requires hard-nosed pragmatism. In future, research funding should be channelled to those institutions and individuals who succeed in converting academic inquiry into commercially exploitable patents as well as Nobel Prizes.

One of the most persistent brakes on Britain's economic performance is our sclerotic planning system, which makes the conversion of agricultural land into commercial and industrial property an exercise of Gothic complexity and horrifying cost. The last government tried to deal with the problem by constraining local authorities' control of planning and imposing regional spatial strategies and the unaccountable Infrastructure Planning Commission. Not only was this undemocratic, it also didn't work.

The coalition has already abolished regional spatial strategies and has promised to restore local democratic control over planning. But what the government's programme currently lacks is a necessary reassertion of the rights of property owners to develop their property as they see fit, without unreasonable interference by any planning authority, whether local, regional or national. If Britain is to achieve the balanced economic growth that all politicians claim to support, we need to make it easier for businesses to set up and expand their operations throughout the country and this will require a wholesale reduction in the burden of regulation that controls what buildings you can build, where you can build them and how.

Elbows out for Britain

There is still a hint of distaste for the dirty business of doing business among Britain's public sector elites. If we are to create the prosperity we will need to afford first-class healthcare and education for everyone in the country, ministers, civil servants and diplomats will need to become a little less polite and a lot more proactive in seeking out opportunities for national profit. Unlike many of its competitors, Britain has operated in a global marketplace for centuries. The Victorians built history's greatest empire off the back of the ingenuity and industry of the British people, massive investment in public infrastructure and a whole-hearted commitment by the British state to help British businesses exploit international trade. The coalition government needs to rediscover this nineteenth-century brashness and, with its elbows out in the world's bazaars, do whatever it takes to help Britain's businesses achieve commercial success.

2. Power to the people

One of the defining stories of the six decades since the Second World War has been the collapse in deference towards people in positions of authority – and for the institutions that they represent. Iconoclasm has not been restricted to the Church of England, whose grip on the consciences of the British people is weaker now than at any time since Henry VIII broke with Rome. It has affected the monarchy, the judiciary and the BBC: indeed any institution which claims that it derives its authority from superior wisdom, morals or breeding. The dominant political force in the country is not socialism or conservatism but a spirit of populist reform similar to that which inspired the Levellers during the Civil War.

In 2009, it was Parliament's turn to be put into the stocks. Some have characterised the scandal over MPs' expenses as a disaster for British democracy. It is certainly true that the litany of petty corruption, and the attempts to use parliamentary privilege to shield it from the public gaze, have obliterated whatever faith the British people retained in the probity of those they send to Parliament. But, even if no-one will now believe in the idea of a dignified parliamentary priesthood, as promoted by Pugin's pseudo-ecclesiastical designs for the interior of Parliament, the events of the last two years promise a wholly benign and long overdue revolution in our political system.

An idea whose time has finally come

Conservatives have been arguing for radical decentralisation of power for nearly ten years. In 2001, in *A Blue Tomorrow*, I argued that a programme of decentralisation 'would demonstrate an approach to leadership, which is in tune with our less deferential age, and recognises that nobody has all the answers.' In 2002, Policy Exchange published *Going Local*, the first report to suggest that police forces should be accountable to directly elected police commissioners, council leaders or mayors. In 2004, we also published *Big Bang Localism*, Simon Jenkins's manifesto for a massive transfer of power and responsibility to local authorities. In 2005, two of the most thoughtful and creative Conservative parliamentarians, Douglas Carswell and Daniel Hannan, launched Direct Democracy, a campaign for radical decentralisation, and recruited a wide range of new Conservative MPs and MEPs to their cause. Many of these MPs are now ministers in the coalition government and many of the policy ideas developed by Policy Exchange and the Direct Democracy campaigners featured in Conservative Party's manifesto at the election and have been retained in the coalition agreement.

Now that our political elites have been declared morally and fiscally bankrupt, it is no longer possible for anyone to argue that the best way to run our country and our communities is for the British people to cast one vote every four or five years and hand over all control to whatever motley collection of individual representatives that this process produces. At a time when people are better educated and better informed than at any point in human history, a political system that gives power to an elect few is simply indefensible. The only way to rebuild respect for our democracy and the institutions of government is to disperse power widely and make decisions as close as possible to the people affected. This is the fundamental purpose of David Cameron's Big Society.

Parliament will not be the only target for this revolution in the way we govern ourselves. Civil servants, though they may peddle the bromide of public consultation, too often share Douglas Jay's view that 'the gentleman in Whitehall really does know better what is good for people than the people know themselves'. Understanding that we should prefer a messy set of arrangements that reflect people's diverging wishes to a rationally planned system that excludes individual choice and community initiative will require a complete transformation in the culture and attitudes of the civil service.

Local government will not be immune either. Although the decentralisation revolution must rein back central government interference in local authorities and boost substantially the range of services for which local government is responsible, the angry heirs of the Levellers will not tolerate local politicians and bureaucrats gleefully picking up where the national ones left off. All branches of government and all organisations in the public sector will need to embrace an intensely democratic ethos, where information available to those in government is shared with the people, on whose behalf they are governing, and where any decisions that can be made by an individual, a family, a community or a voluntary association are left to them, and not grabbed by politicians or bureaucrats claiming to know best.

Which branch of government should do what?

The coalition programme published in May did not envisage the transfer of major new responsibilities to local government, focusing instead on Big Society measures to create opportunities for organisations outside government, and restricting its proposals for local authorities to the removal of national and regional interference in matters such as planning and housing. While these are all steps in the right direction, the coalition programme as a whole underestimates the critical importance of strong and accountable local authorities in stimulating and supporting the growth of the Big Society on the ground. Central government can do some things to give local charities and community groups the power and resources to run local facilities and provide services that people want. But these will usually need to be commissioned or at least partly funded by a democratically accountable branch of government. Central agencies and government departments are simply unable to do this in a way that reflects the specific needs of different local communities. Unless the coalition transfers a wide range of responsibilities to local authorities, and gets them to do the heavy lifting of passing power to charities and voluntary groups, the Big Society will be stillborn.

Deciding which powers should be transferred to local government will not be easy. Even supporters of radical decentralisation do not agree on how to divide up responsibilities between central and local government. In *Big Bang Localism*, Simon Jenkins argued for the NHS to be broken up and health services to be run by counties and cities, while towns and parishes should be charged with caring for 'whatever gives a community its pride and visual character': primary schools and old people's homes, nurseries and day centres, clinics and surgeries, parks and sports centres, libraries and community halls. In *The Plan*, published in 2008, Douglas Carswell and Daniel Hannan argued for local authorities in England and either the Welsh Executive or Welsh local authorities to be given responsibility for all of the matters that have been transferred to the Scottish Executive in the devolution settlement (though they wanted the NHS to be replaced with a Singaporean model of personal health savings accounts, backed up by catastrophic health insurance).

One member of the Cabinet has already announced plans for a much bigger shift in power than was envisaged in the coalition programme. In England, the new Health Secretary, Andrew Lansley, plans to devolve power first to patients and professionals, by giving patients the right to register with any general practice and by transferring of responsibility for commissioning most healthcare to consortia of GPs. After this has happened, the residual functions of primary care trusts and strategic health authorities will be transferred to local authorities, so that they can exploit synergies with the commissioning of social care, for which they are already responsible. Lansley also plans to give local authorities responsibility for commissioning local public health programmes, because he recognises that individual patient choice doesn't really make sense in the context of public health. This combination of decentralisation to individuals and professionals, where possible, and devolution to local authorities, where not, should guide the coalition's approach across the board.

The key distinction is between those responsibilities that involve services delivered to a whole community and those that involve services delivered to individuals or households. Where a service is delivered to an individual or family, we should strengthen the relationship between them and the institution that serves them, giving them the power to choose and the institution the freedom to compete. Services that fall into this category include all mainstream education and healthcare. The patient or parent or student should have as much control as possible over the choice of hospital or school or college. We should remove any artificial limit on the number of providers able to offer their services to them and ensure that all members of the public have access to complete and comparable information about the performance of those competing for their custom. There is no need for local authorities to have a lead role in planning the provision of these services and, where they already do, as in social care, they should be required to everything they can to put decision-making power in the hands of those who need care.

Where a service is provided to the community as a whole, giving individuals or households the ultimate control that comes from having a choice about when and where to get the service is impossible. So the only way of giving people an ability to influence the nature of the service being offered is to make that service the responsibility of a local authority which is run by people elected by members of that community. Services which fall into this category include planning, licensing, the environment, policing, criminal justice, public health, libraries, arts and heritage, sport and leisure.

The principle that local authorities should focus on services delivered to whole communities has some important implications. It explains why it is right for the coalition government to reduce the role of local education authorities and liberate schools from bureaucratic control so that they can focus on meeting the individual expectations of pupils and parents. But it also implies that the coalition should move beyond the halfway house of introducing local police commissioners and transfer the responsibility for policing and criminal justice (including the court service, the prison service and rehabilitation, resettlement and probation services) to elected local authorities.

He who calls the tune should pay the piper

Giving local authorities responsibility for policing and criminal justice will help give people a sense of control over what happens in their local communities. But, on their own, local elections cannot make these key community services truly accountable. It is easy to get people to support an increase in police numbers or a prison-building programme if they are not going to have to foot the bill. That is why the Conservative government should exploit current fiscal pressures to cut central grant funding for local government services and increase local authorities' freedom to raise a range of local taxes. While local tax decisions only affect a quarter of the revenues that fund local services, democratic accountability will be severely distorted. When every local authority is raising more than half of the money it needs from locally determined taxes, voters will be presented with a true picture of the costs and benefits of their decisions. Giving people control does not only mean that they should be in the driving seat. It also means that they should be the ones who have to pay to fill the car up with petrol.

In *The Plan*, Carswell and Hannan proposed the wholesale replacement of VAT with a local sales tax, to be determined and collected by local authorities, and pointed out that VAT conveniently raises almost exactly the same amount as the total central government grant to local authorities. In a series of reports for Policy Exchange, published in 2004, Tony Travers and Lorena Esposito argued that local authorities should have a range of taxes at their disposal and proposed a hybrid solution, involving an end to central government capping of council tax, the restoration to local authorities of control over business rates (although they would not be allowed to increase business rates by a higher percentage than council tax) and the allocation to local authorities of a portion of national income tax collected in their area (4 per cent of the basic rate) and the freedom to vary the rate up to a maximum of 6 per cent or down to zero.

As the last Conservative government discovered, changes to local taxation are fraught with political danger. It would be suicide for the coalition government to propose a change that immediately creates large numbers of winners and losers, as the winners will quietly pocket their gains, while the losers will howl with fury and take to the streets in protest. But that is not an excuse for inaction. The coalition agreement envisages a review of possible reforms to local government finance. The last thing we need is a repeat of the Lyons Review, commissioned by Gordon Brown, which spent a very long time coming to no clear conclusion. The team leading the new review should be charged with producing, within twelve months, proposals that would enable all local authorities to raise at least 50 per cent of their budgets through locally determined taxation, without creating large numbers of immediate losers.

Is local government up to the job?

Few people in modern politics admit to being unashamed centralisers but many give vent to serious concerns about the competence and leadership of local government – and use this as an excuse for sticking with the status quo. While local authorities are, as a rule, better managed than central government agencies, few of them boast strong political or executive leadership. This is, in part, a result of decades in which local authorities' freedom for manoeuvre has been squeezed. But that does nothing to alter the fact that a dramatic transfer of responsibility to local government might put intolerable strain on limited capabilities and undermine the public's confidence in the move towards a less centralised way of running things. The coalition government should therefore take advantage of the fact that it brings together the two biggest parties in local government to propose major reforms of the structure and leadership of local authorities and legislate for their implementation in advance of the transfer of major additional powers.

The reform should start by dealing with the problem of district councils, as 'shire districts' are usually known. Conservative MPs tend to avoid criticism of their role because so many of our most loyal and hard-working supporters are themselves district councillors. But we need to be honest with ourselves and the British people. Shire districts were invented in 1972; they are not an ancient feature of Britain's constitutional landscape. They have taken power away from town and parish councils, and introduced an additional layer of bureaucracy and cost, that cannot be justified, when we are imposing painful cuts across the public sector. Nobody in Britain feels a surge of pride when the name of their district is mentioned. In my own constituency, people feel an attachment to their county of Lincolnshire, to their town of Grantham, Stamford or Bourne, or to their village. South Kesteven District Council is relatively well managed and maintains one of the lowest council taxes in the country; but few of the people it serves would mourn its passing.

The coalition should abolish shire districts, passing most of their powers down to town and parish councils and transferring those responsibilities that affect a wider area to county councils. This would save money on offices and administrative overheads and would restore to towns and villages the right to decide (and the responsibility to pay for) the future of vital local facilities like museums, leisure centres and parks. Cities should continue to be governed by metropolitan boroughs, although the name should change to 'city council' and their leadership and governance should be changed as set out below.

The coalition should act to strengthen the leadership of all local authorities – and their scrutiny by democratic representatives. Directly elected executive leaders or mayors should be introduced to all local authorities (parishes, towns, counties and cities) and be empowered to appoint a small cabinet to help run the authority. The role of elected councillors should be to represent their residents' interests and hold the executive to account.

Some people will argue that these reforms would themselves represent a huge imposition by central government on local communities. But so does the structure that we have inherited. Far from being the organic expression of hundreds of years of local feeling, it is the cobbled-together creation of a series of previous governments, and it is too feeble to bear the weight of the responsibilities that true localists want local government to take on.

Britain's Big Bang will require a strong foundation or it will blow up in our faces and condemn Britain to the horrors of central planning for decades to come.

Putting people in charge

Strong and accountable local authorities, which have assumed responsibility for a much wider range of services, should then be charged with stimulating and supporting the development of a flourishing Big Society in the communities they represent. While central government should not be allowed to impose requirements on the precise nature of the services being delivered by local authorities, it should legislate to require all branches of government, central and local, to give people a real handle on the services on which they rely, and to maximise opportunities for independent charities, voluntary organisations and neighbourhood groups to take responsibility for improving local communities. There are three main ways to do this.

Information

The first is information. Back in 1937, when Douglas Jay first wrote that line about the superior wisdom of the gentleman in Whitehall, there was a kernel of truth in his observation. To the extent that civil servants had a monopoly of information, it is also true that they were in a better position to make judgements than most members of the public, who were necessarily ignorant of the likely consequences and costs of the different courses of action open to government. This is no longer the case.

Nowadays, there is no technical reason why all the information available to a senior council officer or government minister cannot be shared with the public. So our approach to the release of information needs to be turned on its head. We should abandon the current bureaucratic approach, where civil servants or politicians determine which information will be most useful (or least harmful) and require providers to report solely on the defined measures. Instead, there should be a presumption that all information produced for internal consumption should be shared with the public, unless there are strong reasons to the contrary.

Everyone will accept that the interests of national security, personal privacy or child protection may require some information to be kept confidential. But this should be justified in every instance and not allowed to act as a blanket shielding huge areas of government activity from scrutiny. In this new era of transparency, the coalition government should mandate the publication of all other information according to open data standards that make it consistent, accurate and comparable with the data collected by other institutions operating in the same field. It can then be left to independent organisations and individuals to analyse the information in whichever way they think is most revealing. Even if few people will have the time or inclination to sift through mountains of data, intermediaries will spring up to do the donkey work and present clear summaries of the relevant facts to assist people's decisions.

There are several different types of information that are important sources of control for the public. The first is information about what is happening in a local area. Such information, which may relate to the incidence of problems (such as crime, vandalism or the breakdown in public infrastructure) or the availability of services (such as street cleaning, rubbish collection and public transport), is often best displayed in maps. Maps give people information about the state of their community and make it possible for them to compare their lot with those of neighbouring communities. Armed with this information, they can highlight trouble hotspots or gaps in services, campaign for public resources to be shifted from areas of abundance to areas of need or organise voluntary initiatives like litter squads and neighbourhood watch schemes to sort problems out.

The second type of information is data about the results achieved by different providers of any service. Every organisation supplying services to the public collects information about their own performance, recording the outcome of every course or treatment or shift, the time it took and the money it cost. If objective performance data of this kind is published according to open standards, and then combined with personal reviews by previous users, people will be able to draw sophisticated conclusions about which organisation is offering the best value for money, the most rapid response or the most personal service and then make judgements about which of them will best suit their needs.

The third type of information relates to public decision-making processes. Members of the public have a right to know who ministers, parliamentarians and public officials are meeting as they are forming their views about an issue and to read the contracts committing public money to major projects or programmes. Politicians need to be able to have confidential conversations with each other, with their advisors and with the officials who support them. But, as far as possible, their communications with people and organisations outside government should be shared with the public in whose interest they are working. This will not only give members of the public the information they need to challenge key government decisions. The prospect of publication will also tend to keep politicians and officials honest, by giving them an incentive to restrict their dealings with lobbyists and other representatives of special interests to a minimum.

Ownership

The second great source of control is ownership. Until 1979, the prevailing view in Britain was that state ownership was the best way to give the broad mass of people a stake in the most valuable assets in society. People did not need to own their own home, because the council would own them on their behalf and let them live in them. They did not need to own stocks and shares, because the government would nationalise the major industries and manage them in the public interest. They did not need to own their own pensions, because the government would fund a state pension for every citizen and pay for it by taxing the better off.

What we discovered was that state ownership flattens, deadens and homogenises. Denying people's individuality, initiative and independence of spirit, it strips them of both power and responsibility. Reminding them of their dependence on others for all of the things which men and women are genetically programmed to try and win for themselves, it shreds their self-respect. The reason Margaret Thatcher's policy of giving council house tenants the right to buy had such a massive impact was because it reforged the connection between working people and the fundamental human urge to provide shelter for your family.

The ownership revolution, which Margaret Thatcher began, stalled during Britain's wasted decade, because Labour has never shrugged off its instinctive belief that state ownership is the fairest way to organise the distribution of assets. Political expediency may have prevented them from seeking to reverse the privatisation of the nationalised industries and the sale of council houses but the deepest prejudices of their party would never have allowed them to engage in a further transfer of assets out of the state's hands.

The coalition government must restart the ownership revolution and take it into new territory. As well as encouraging people to buy their own home, save for their old age and build up assets to pass on to the next generation, the government should press ahead with its plan to put public assets like playing fields, parks, youth clubs and swimming baths into the hands of voluntary organisations, charities and community groups, who will run them in the interest of local users. By requiring local authorities to transfer the ownership of key community facilities to local trusts, subject to guarantees that they will remain open for all members of the community, we can give those people who have the closest and most consistent connection with a facility the power to organise its upkeep, use and further development.

If ownership can motivate people to invest in and take care of a house, a park or a village hall, then it can also motivate employees to improve the productivity of the organisation they work for and enhance the quality of the service they provide. That's why Conservatives have embraced the co-operative tradition exemplified by the John Lewis Partnership. The coalition wants to encourage employees in hospitals, schools, social work organisations and a wide range of other public sector entities to convert their organisations into independent co-operative enterprises that operate under simple payment-by-results contracts and can replace the suffocating embrace of micromanagement by Whitehall with genuine freedom to do things in new ways.

Circle Health provides one model. It was set up, and is owned and run by, clinicians who 'believe that the collective intelligence of the network of many will always be smarter than any small group of executives'. Through its new 'compact' hospitals, Circle is demonstrating that, contrary to the propaganda emanating from instinctively centralising strategic health authorities and large hospital trusts, it is possible to run small district hospitals efficiently and provide an excellent local service to patients.

Choice

The third source of control is choice. If the people running state-funded schools had to 'compete for pupils', if they knew that the parents of all their actual and potential pupils had complete information about the results they achieve and had several schools to choose from, they would have a clear incentive to understand what parents really want. They would make sure that they offer the exams and extracurricular activities that parents prefer, would motivate their good teachers to excel, chivvy the mediocre ones to improve and force the bad ones to move on. Currently, parents are in the worst of all possible worlds, as they are given lots of information about different schools' performance through league tables and Ofsted reports, but then have very little power to choose the school that best suits their child. Instead of focusing on satisfying parents' wants and children's needs, local education authorities treat their schools as assembly lines in a huge manufacturing plant and their overriding priority is to manage the allocation of pupils to schools so as to 'balance the lines'. As a result, good schools are prevented from adding more places in order to protect failing schools with spare capacity. And naturally ambitious parents who just want the best for their child are told that they must sacrifice their offspring's interests on the altar of 'surplus places' and 'fair admissions'.

For the power of choice to have any meaning, it must be easy for a successful head teacher to expand a good school and easy for groups of parents as well as education businesses and charities to set up new schools and claim their fair share of state funding for any pupils they recruit. School choice will remain a tantalising shibboleth until parents have more schools to choose from. But, once they do, the act of choosing the best school for their child will create a bond of commitment between parents and schools that will encourage more parents to get involved in their children's education. Nothing would do more to improve Britain's education performance than that.

The same lessons about choice could be applied to many other public services. Giving users a genuine choice between different GPs, different hospitals, different care homes, different further education colleges would encourage competing providers to increase their productivity and improve the quality of the services they offer.

A British constitution

If the new government wants to make the decentralisation of power irreversible, we must codify the rights of the individual in relation to all branches of government as well as the division of responsibilities between central and local government. These provisions should be enshrined in law, with a super-majority in both Houses of Parliament required to overturn or amend it. Having done so, the Speaker of the House of Commons should then rule out of order any questions on matters that are the responsibility of elected local authorities, as is currently the case with matters devolved to the Scottish Parliament and Welsh Assembly. Only then will we be able to resist the centralising impulses of ministers, who will always demand control over matters for which they are being blamed, and civil servants, who want to impose a neat, rational order on the chaos of local diversity.

Thatcherite Conservatives have tended to focus on the size of the state, as measured by the percentage of GDP consumed by public spending and tax. Liberal Conservatives are more interested in the power of the state and its lack of accountability. If the coalition can entrench a new constitutional settlement which disperses government responsibilities more widely, vests much greater power in accountable local authorities, and ensures that all branches of government give as much control as possible to the people using their services and real autonomy to those working to provide them, it will have done something much more important than reducing the size of the state as a share of GDP. It will have turned our government into what it should be: the servant of the people, not its master.

3. Using deficit reduction to drive

radical reform

If the mission of the new coalition government is to lead Britain up a hard road to a sunny mountaintop, then Britain's budget deficit looms like an enormous boulder blocking the path and threatens to make progress on all other issues impossible. It is true that dealing with the deficit will be an enormous task and will soak up much of the energy of the new government. But we must not allow it to distract us from the other radical changes required to tackle the social, economic and security challenges facing Britain. In fact, we should use the fiscal crisis as our ally in making the case for dramatic change in the way decisions are made, services are delivered and communities are run.

Some will say it is naïve to think that you can reform the way we do things and save money at the same time – but we must stop our ears to such defeatism. It is what every successful business has been doing over the last twenty years and it is past time for all branches of government to catch up. Understanding customers' wants and needs, removing layers of management, cutting out inefficient processes, incentivising individual and team performance, supporting innovation and holding people to account for their actions – these are the tools that have transformed the productivity of great British companies such as GlaxoSmithkline, Tesco, Vodafone and Rolls-Royce. The fiscal crisis offers a once-in-a-generation opportunity to use the same tools to transform our public sector.

Understanding the problem

It is very hard to convey the scale of Britain's budget deficit and the effect it is having on our national debt. A government deficit of £155,000,000,000 being added to a debt of £1,000,000,000,000; 11 per cent on top of 60 per cent of national income. What do these numbers really mean? And why do they matter?

Although countries do not face exactly the same constraints as households or businesses, it helps us understand our current fiscal position if we translate these impenetrably vast numbers into more human terms. Imagine for a moment that you used to earn £10,000 as a part-time secretary and your partner used to earn £40,000 as a manager in a car dealership. Since the recession, your hours have been cut. Your partner's employer has gone into receivership and the only job he has been able to find is as a sales rep in another dealership. As a result, your combined income has fallen from £50,000 to £44,000. The good news is that your mortgage, at £30,000 or 60 per cent of your original combined income, is not excessive and interest rates are low. But your monthly bills are outstripping your reduced take-home pay and in the last year you have built up debts of £6,000 on your credit cards. Your partner seems totally unconcerned. But it is giving you sleepless nights and, over breakfast one morning, the two of you have a blazing row about the action you should take to get back into the black.

In the end, you agree to go and see your bank manager to ask for a loan so you can pay off your credit card debt. He needs to understand your situation so that he can assess your credit-worthiness. He asks: 'Are your jobs secure? Are you expecting pay rises next year? Are you planning to start a family any time soon? Do you have any elderly relatives who might depend on you for financial support?' Your partner starts to brag about the bonus he is bound to get this Christmas and a promotion that is just round the corner. But, on further questioning, he reveals that the business where he works is having a tough year and has just laid off a member of staff. The bank manager raises an eyebrow and asks what cutbacks you would be willing to make – not just to bring your spending back into line with your lower after-tax income but to give you a bit of headroom so you can meet your loan repayments. After your partner protests, a hint of steel enters the bank manager's tone and he makes clear that he will not extend a loan, unless you give up one of your cars and cancel the new kitchen you have just ordered.

When it comes to Britain's deficit and debt, the bond markets are the government's bank manager. In deciding what interest rate is needed to compensate for the risk of lending the British government money, they are constantly asking the same sort of questions a bank manager would. What level of growth can Britain reasonably predict in the next few years? To what extent will tax revenues automatically bounce back as the economy grows? Are we facing any long-term increases in costs as a result of an ageing population, immigration or shifts in energy prices?

Until George Osborne's emergency Budget, the bond markets had good reason to feel nervous about Britain's credit-worthiness. The vast indebtedness hanging over individuals, families and businesses has forced them all to cut spending to reduce their debts. Even as exports and business investment pick up some of the slack, this process is likely to produce pretty anaemic economic growth for the next couple of years. Low growth will inevitably depress corporation tax, capital gains tax, VAT and income tax revenues and there is no way that tax revenues from the financial sector, which funded a large part of government spending in the last ten years, will ever return on their previous scale. Most of what economists call the 'structural deficit' is a result of this permanent drop in tax revenues after the financial crisis and recession.

Without radical action, prospects for controlling the costs facing the government would also be bleak. Britain's population is ageing and the demands for health and social care will increase, as will the cost of new treatments and technologies. After several years of falling school rolls, we are also about to face an increase in numbers of school-age children.

The combination of a permanent fall in tax revenues and long-term pressure on costs means that we cannot simply wait for the budget deficit to close automatically over the next phase of the economic cycle. Like the bank manager, bond investors need the government to have a clear plan to bring its costs back down to less than its income – and to stick to it. Their treatment of Greece, Spain and Portugal showed that they would punish any hesitancy or backsliding with an increase in the long-term rates that households pay on their mortgages and businesses pay on their loans.

The emergency Budget

The emergency Budget that George Osborne unveiled on 22 June 2010 was truly radical. It laid the foundations for the revival of private enterprise with a bold plan for yearly cuts in corporation tax. It protected the least well off with an increase in the tax-free allowance for basic rate income taxpayers and an increase in the child tax credit. It also set a clear direction for the public finances and did much to reassure the bond markets of the UK's long-term creditworthiness. But it will not be easy to deliver. Although announcing tax rises, like the increase in VAT and capital gains tax, requires great political nerve, implementing them is not difficult. Parliament passes the necessary clauses in the Finance Bill and the increases just happen. Cutting public spending is not so easy and the Liberal–Conservative government is relying on spending cuts for over 70 per cent of deficit reduction over the next five years, implying an average of 25 per cent cuts in real terms over five years for those departments that are not protected (i.e. all except Health and International Development.)

Achieving these savings will be very challenging. It requires radical surgery, not just a close shave. It will not be enough for the Comprehensive Spending Review just to assign new, lower, budget numbers to existing departments, services and programmes. We need a fundamental restructuring of the way government is organised if we are to have any chance of maintaining high-quality public services while dramatically cutting their cost.

Big bang localism

In the previous chapter, I argued that the coalition should transfer responsibility for a wide range of services and government activities to local authorities. This Big Bang reform would make it possible to dismantle some of central government's most wasteful bureaucracies. Until now, advocates of radical decentralisation have tended to rely on moral arguments about the undemocratic nature of rule by the central state. The fiscal crisis provides a more compelling reason to devolve large chunks of government responsibility to the local level: we have run out of money. The only way of meeting the Chancellor's public expenditure targets without slashing the services delivered to the public will be to engineer a complete redesign of services that breaks down the divisions between health, housing, welfare and policing, and focuses on the whole package of services delivered to each individual and family.

A reconfiguration of this kind cannot be implemented centrally. The central agencies are too big and each of them is dealing with too many people to allow for the flexibility and inventiveness that will be required to integrate services while cutting costs. Furthermore, there isn't going to be one right way of doing things. Different combinations of services may make sense in different areas. Building on the lessons of the last government's Total Place pilots, we should encourage local authorities to back local priorities and experiment with home-grown solutions.

In the last chapter, I argued that we need a new constitutional settlement in which local government has unfettered responsibility for all services that are delivered to communities rather than to individuals. There may be other areas where it might make sense to divide the responsibility for making decisions about policy, which should remain with central government, from the responsibility to deliver services to individuals, which could be passed to local authorities. The Department for Work and Pensions' role in the benefits system, for example, might be restricted to determining what benefits should exist and broad rules about who should receive them under what circumstances. Meanwhile, the assessment of individuals' circumstances and the administration of benefit payments might be passed to local authorities, who could then merge this function with the teams responsible for administering housing benefit and council tax benefit.

In every area where central government functions are being transferred to local government, the Comprehensive Spending Review should specify the additional amount of central government funding that will transferred to local authorities, after the spending cuts have been taken into account. But the government should also make it clear that, while these services continue to be funded by central government grant, all additional grants will be rolled up into each local authority's block grant, so that local leaders have genuine freedom to reconfigure services as they see fit. Only if they can pool budgets, merge back offices, redesign processes and commission services jointly with other local authorities and public bodies will local authorities be able to squeeze out better services for much less money. In these straitened times, trusting local initiative is not a luxury but a financial necessity.

Open to offers

While the Treasury should not restrict local authorities' freedom to innovate by tying particular elements of central government grant to particular services, it should impose a few general rules governing the way in which taxpayers' money should be spent by any and all branches of the public sector. The first of these should require the commissioning of any service funded by Treasury grant to be subject to competitive review every few years. Any organisation (public, private, co-operative, community owned or charitable) should have the right to submit proposals and the commissioning authority should not be allowed to impose overly prescriptive service specifications, so that competing suppliers are free to propose the radical redesign of local services. Furthermore, the commissioning authority should be required to publish in full their assessment of the proposals made by alternative providers and their reasons for deciding to adopt one proposal rather than another. This will help ensure that all branches of government are genuinely open to offers from those who think that they could do a better job of serving the public.

Payment by results

The Treasury should also require all branches of government to maximise the use of payment mechanisms that link the expenditure of taxpayers' money to achievement of concrete results. In recent years, the NHS has introduced tariffs setting a standard cost for particular treatments. This makes it possible to measure the productivity of different hospitals and treatment centres – and to drive down unit costs for, say, a hernia operation or a knee replacement to the level achieved by the most efficient providers. The coalition government is already committed to introducing payment by results to the welfare system, so that an organisation that helps get someone back into work is paid the bulk of its compensation after the client has completed several months in his or her new job. The Justice Secretary, Ken Clarke, is also keen to introduce payment by results to the prisons and probation services, so that those responsible for managing prisons and delivering rehabilitation and resettlement services are rewarded when an ex-offender avoids reoffending for more than two years.

Payment by results can be applied most easily to services which are delivered in standard units, or which bring about a measurable change in the circumstances of a particular individual. It is harder to see how a tariff could be constructed to reflect the cost of a fire brigade fighting a fire, since fires are not standard and much of the value provided by a fire brigade is in assisting prevention and giving people reassurance by being on standby. But, even if it is difficult to conceive of a system of tariffs to price some services, it will almost always be possible to think of some concrete results that the service provider should be aiming to achieve – and to link at least part of the payment for the service to this. So, in the case of a fire brigade, it might be possible to make a small but significant proportion of their funding conditional on a reduction in the number of deaths and major injuries caused by fire.

Innovation

When the United States faced its worst economic crisis, President Franklin Roosevelt demanded 'bold, persistent experimentation', saying: 'It is common sense to take a method and try it: if it fails, admit it frankly and try another. But above all, try something.' This is the culture we need to foster throughout the public sector. Successful companies will dedicate a few per cent of turnover every year to investment in innovation. And they don't cut this during tough times – in fact, the best ones lean into the wind, because they know that the only sure way to survive the ferment of capitalism that Schumpeter described as creative destruction is to innovate more, and more successfully, than your competitors.

Government does this very badly, where it does it at all. The prevailing attitude in our public sector is one of risk avoidance. Civil servants and public sector managers are behaving entirely rationally when they observe that it is better for their careers (and makes for a quieter life) to carry on trying to make incremental improvements to an inherited system, however inefficient and unresponsive, rather than dare to do things differently and run the risk of failing in the attempt. They lack the skills, the incentives (of which more later) and, crucially, the support of ministers and permanent secretaries to make relentless innovation a core part of the way they do their jobs.

There are a few simple things the coalition government can do to entrench innovation in the way the public sector is run. Like Ken Clarke, ministers should pose questions in a way that challenge the status quo: not how do we run the prisons service, but what do we want prisoners to be doing while they are detained at Her Majesty's pleasure? The new Efficiency and Reform Group, bringing together the Cabinet Office and the Treasury, could insist that every department and every agency allocate a specific proportion of its budget to innovation and account for it to the group and to a parliamentary select committee. They can make a commitment to innovation one of the key measures of the performance of civil servants and managers and back that up with incentives.

But we need to be realistic: it will take years to create a new culture in the public sector and to develop the mindset and aptitudes to harvest the fruits of innovation. In the meantime, we need to put money and political clout behind organisations with track records of innovation in the public interest: one of the best is Participle, which in the Southwark Circle has already created a remarkable network of mutual support for the over-50s, using older people's spare time, goodwill and innate sociability to combat loneliness and reduce the likelihood that vulnerable people will end up in hospital or needing more expensive forms of social care. Ministers should encourage other local authorities to take up successful innovations like the Circle. They should also steer the handsomely funded National Endowment for Science, Technology and the Arts to spend less money on staff (£7 million out of a total expenditure of £25.5 million in 2009) and instead commission outside organisations such as Participle to develop new kinds of services in areas where current arrangements are ineffective or unaffordable, and to seed-fund pilots of these innovative solutions with forward-looking councils.

Incentives make the world go round

The process of cutting public spending while maintaining or improving service levels will require radical change in almost all parts of the public sector – and demand the ingenuity, application and goodwill of thousands of public servants. That's why it is essential that the government follow the example of every successful business and introduce a system of incentives that flows throughout the public sector and offers employees at every level a stake in the successful transformation of the organisations in which they work.

The incentives system should combine three currencies that are valued, in some measure, by all human beings: power, money and recognition. The Treasury should establish a simple and clear system of financial incentives for departments. Once a department has achieved a required minimum level of savings (say 5 per cent per annum), the Treasury should allow the department to retain a quarter of any savings over and above the minimum and invest 80 per cent of that quarter into programmes selected by the department's board (giving the departmental leadership the power to back their own priorities). The other 20 per cent of any additional savings retained by the department should flow into a bonus pool, for distribution to teams and individuals based on the assessment of their performance by those to whom they report.

In parallel, the Cabinet Office should create a recognition system based on the distribution of honours. Automatic award of honours on the appointment to specific positions should be stopped and replaced with the award of honours based on the recommendation of customers, managers or colleagues. It should be possible for a middle manager in Jobcentre Plus who designs a new training scheme that is rolled out across the network and helps thousands of people back into work to get a knighthood – even when his better-paid boss, the chief executive of Jobcentre Plus, is still plain Mister or Ms.

Buying the basics

The great irony of Britain's centralised state is that, while Labour ministers spent thirteen years trying to dictate the precise shape of how services were delivered in every hospital and school and to specify the exact way in which each provider should be organised, they made little or no attempt to control the costs of generic inputs like IT, stationery or invoice-processing. We live in a country where central government prescribes a huge proportion of what every maths teacher in the country must teach but where nobody cares that every hospital buys its own selection of scalpels, every quango installs its own IT network and the cost of handling a cheque can be multiples higher in government than in the private sector. In this Alice-in-Wonderland world, those things that should be managed very loosely are subject to rigid central controls. And, those things that should be managed tightly are left to a chaotic and catastrophically wasteful free-for-all.

In future, the Treasury should require all publicly funded organisations to buy standard office supplies and equipment as well as basic ICT services like PC networks and data storage from centrally approved suppliers. They should also require them to report the unit cost of basic administrative processes – and should cut their funding by whatever amount they are spending more than a benchmark cost for each process.

Sweat the assets

Private sector organisations operating expensive capital equipment or occupying valuable premises are always looking for ways to sweat their assets. Budget airlines have transformed their processes to make it possible for each expensive plane to do several trips a day. Engineering companies work three shifts on their most expensive machines. They do this because they are paying the capital cost of their assets and the capital cost is the same every hour of every day, whether the asset is being used or lying idle. The same disciplines do not operate in the public sector. Government departments do not pay rent, in cash, at market prices, on the property they occupy, so they have no incentive to rationalise office space and reduce the average number of square feet per employee or the average cost per square foot. Because public sector organisations usually have to make separate applications for capital funding and do not have to fund investments in new equipment out of their operating budgets, they don't have an incentive to extend the hours in which the equipment is in use. If we want to get maximum value out of taxpayers' money, we need to ensure that all public sector organisations confront the full cash cost of the assets they use, and are no longer allowed a free ride on the back of the balance sheet they inherited. There has been a huge amount of public investment in the last ten years; the new government needs to make sure that the public is getting the maximum use out of the assets they paid for.

There is a particular opportunity to rationalise government property. The coalition government should transfer the ownership of all the freeholds and head leases of property owned and occupied by the public sector to a central property holding company and require government departments and agencies to pay commercial rents in cash out of their departmental budgets. This would incentivise the public sector to save money by reducing the amount of space per employee, getting different organisations to share offices, subletting spare space and moving offices out of expensive property in central London to cheaper locations. The management of the property holding company should be put up for tender and the winning bidder should be paid according to its results in reducing the total government spend on rent and maximising the proceeds from disposals of surplus property.

Tax increases that do more than just raise money

In his emergency Budget, the Chancellor chose to raise additional tax revenue by increasing VAT and capital gains tax (while cutting corporation tax and increasing the tax-free allowance for basic rate income taxpayers.) Given the urgency of the need for additional revenues and the constraints of the coalition agreement with the Liberal Democrats, this was the right course. But, over the next few years, the government has the opportunity to make further tax reforms that could make it easier to raise the tax-free allowance for the low paid or cut corporation tax yet further, while addressing some of the other challenges that we face.

Tax changes can play a part in helping revive people's faith in local politics. In the last chapter, I argued that the grotesque concentration of power at the centre of our political system is one of the main sources of people's current alienation from politics. Westminster and Whitehall maintain suffocating control over every aspect of the way communities develop and public services are delivered. So it is not surprising that most people see local elections as a waste of time and refuse to take part in a process that has almost no impact on any of the important decisions that affect their lives.

One of the most important ways through which local leaders are emasculated and forced to dance to Whitehall's tune is money. The bulk of the funding for the services provided by local government is derived from central government grants that are disbursed with myriad strings attached. Meanwhile, local business rates are controlled from the centre and our local property tax, the council tax, is regularly capped by ministers.

The coalition government should strengthen the autonomy

of locally elected leaders and reduce their dependence on central government grants. In the Comprehensive Spending Review, George Osborne should announce that there will be a gradual shift away from central government grants towards local taxation over the next five years and that, by 2015/16, all local authorities will be expected to raise at least 50 per cent of the money they spend from local taxation. The money saved by the Treasury should then be used to make further progress on reducing corporation tax and increasing the tax-free allowance for the low paid.

There are a number of ways that local authorities could be given greater financial autonomy. The most radical decentralising step would be to give them the freedom to raise whatever taxes they choose – and then justify their choices to local people at local elections. However, the Chancellor might be reluctant to let local leaders undermine his strategy of cutting corporate taxes to support business investment and growth. An alternative approach would be to specify a range of alternative new taxes that local authorities could introduce – and require specific local tax proposals to be set out in the different parties' local manifestos in advance of the next local elections, so that the voters are given the chance to express their views on the different packages of local taxes proposed. In their report published by Policy Exchange, Tony Travers and Lorena Esposito suggested a gradual approach, which I outlined in the previous chapter.

The pressure to raise revenues to solve the fiscal crisis also presents an opportunity to tackle two of the most important security challenges that Britain faces – our reliance on fossil fuels supplied by countries that are either unscrupulous or downright hostile and our vulnerability to the effects of global warming and climate change. What we should do to address these threats is discussed in detail in Chapter 6. One of the most important measures proposed is the introduction of a carbon tax. Initially, this would simply replace the climate change levy but, over time, it should be steadily increased to around £20 per tonne, so that it makes a substantial contribution to the funding required for major energy infrastructure such as gas storage, smart grids and nuclear waste decommissioning, and provides an increasingly strong price signal to encourage both a cut in energy consumption and increased investment in nuclear and renewable energy supplies.

What if recovery falters?

In recent months, leading members of the Labour Party have predicted a double-dip recession so often that you could be forgiven for thinking that they are secretly hoping for one. All the signs before this book went to press were that modest economic growth was being maintained. But a double-dip recession remains possible. Britain is an open economy, heavily reliant on international trade, and we cannot exclude the possibility that we will be dragged down by a fall in global demand. If this were to happen, what should the coalition government do?

The biggest mistake would be to abandon the coalition's plans to cut current spending on benefits and public services or increase taxes. While the implementation of spending cuts and tax rises will be painful for many individuals and testing for the government, the credibility of the coalition depends on sticking to them – as do the low interest rates we currently enjoy. But that does not mean that there is nothing the government could do to boost demand in a double-dip recession. Even while ministers are bearing down on the long-term structural elements of public expenditure, the Chancellor could offer additional investment tax credits for businesses, boost spending on government guarantees for export finance and provide rebates on employer national insurance. However, any such measures should be explicitly temporary and the legislation to introduce them should provide for their automatic termination once there have been two quarters of growth in excess of, say, an annualised 1 per cent.

Sticking to Treasury knitting

Gordon Brown turned the Treasury from a narrowly focused ministry of finance, charged with maintaining macroeconomic stability and balancing the budget, into a central command structure, like Gosplan, directing the full panoply of Labour's ambitious programmes of economic and social engineering. It should therefore come as no great surprise that the ill-disciplined and incontinent institution that Brown created ended up presiding over the near collapse of the financial system, the deepest recession since the 1930s and the explosion of Britain's budget deficit to over 10 per cent of GDP. George Osborne has rightly pledged to put the Treasury's blinkers back on and focus his department on two core tasks: restoring financial stability by reforming our system of regulation and bringing the budget back into balance by cutting public spending.

This mission, at once new and wholly traditional, gives the Treasury a chance to make amends for the mistakes it made during the era of imperial overreach. Lest any of Osborne's officials regret the passing of their days as omnipotent commissars, he can point out that the successful resolution of our fiscal crisis will have far more revolutionary effects on the way Britain's society, economy and government work than any of the grandiose schemes piloted by Gordon Brown.

4. Healing the wounds of a divided society

There are parts of Glasgow in which nearly 40 per cent of children grow up in homes where there is no adult in paid employment and male life expectancy is lower than in Gaza. When you consider this and set it against the life on display on the streets of Notting Hill and Alderley Edge, it isn't surprising to learn that income inequality in Britain is at its highest level since comparable statistics began in 1961. But that doesn't make it any the less shocking.

Britain has made good progress in abolishing absolute poverty in the past 100 years. The combination of taxpayer-financed healthcare, free primary and secondary education and a wide range of benefits for people who are out of work, disabled or living on very low incomes mean that there is no reason for any British citizen to go without their basic material needs being met. But this reduction in absolute poverty has been accompanied by a big increase in inequality in our country. The salaries of the richest have soared, while the wages of those at the bottom have stagnated. This has led to a situation in which the wealthiest 10 per cent in Britain are about 100 times richer than the poorest 10 per cent.

The effects of inequality

The free market right has traditionally argued that unequal outcomes don't matter, so long as people have an equal opportunity to succeed, society as a whole is becoming better off and the basic needs of the vulnerable are guaranteed by the welfare state. But this view has recently been challenged by two academics, Richard Wilkinson and Kate Pickett. In their recent book, *The Spirit Level*, they seek to demonstrate that inequality has a major impact on a country's general wellbeing and undermines the quality of life of even the richest people in it. They present data which suggests that inequality is a key factor in explaining Britain's high levels of obesity, crime, teenage pregnancy, illiteracy and addiction. They argue that inequality gets under the skin, causing people intense stress about their status in relation to others and breaking down levels of trust between people. People at the bottom feel worthless, those in the middle are envious of those above, and those at the top are paranoid about losing their place. This leads them to argue that if Britain became as equal as Japan, Norway, Sweden and Finland,

> levels of trust might be expected to be two-thirds as high again as they are now, mental illness might be more than halved, everyone would get an additional year of life, teenage birth rates could fall to one-third of what they are now, homicide rates could fall by 75 per cent, everyone could get the equivalent of almost seven weeks extra holiday a year, and the government could be closing prisons all over the country.

But is it really that simple? We should start by analysing the logic of the argument set out in *The Spirit Level*. Fundamentally, it is an economic one. They have analysed the causal links between an economic measure, income inequality, and a whole range of behavioural outcomes. Having established that the link is strong, they then conclude that economic measures to reduce income inequality will lead to a reduction in dysfunctional behaviour. But this begs several questions. Firstly, can we really trust the statistics? Secondly, can we be sure that it is income inequality itself that causes low levels of trust and the resulting social problems – might it not be something else that is either closely correlated with income inequality or is its underlying cause? Thirdly, even if the rise in income inequality has caused a breakdown in trust, is it clear that trust would be rebuilt if income inequality were reduced? And, fourthly, can we be certain that the factors that produce low income inequality in Scandinavia and Japan are replicable in Britain and, if they are, that they would be sufficient to deliver the same benign social outcomes?

A recent Policy Exchange report claims that there are serious flaws in Wilkinson and Pickett's statistical analysis. The author asserts that 'the statistical analysis . . . is heavily flawed' and ignores the 'cultural patterns that are often generating their findings'. For example, 'the association between a country's homicide rate and its level of income inequality depends entirely on the high murder rate in the USA (which probably has more to do with its gun control laws than its income distribution)'. Similarly, the link between average life expectancy and income inequality 'rests entirely on the longevity of people in Japan', which may have more to do with their diet or their genes.

In Scandinavia, it is certainly true that people pay higher taxes and support higher benefits for the less well off. But it is also true that most people are better educated. Furthermore, until recently, Scandinavian countries did not undergo high levels of immigration so their populations have tended to be much more homogeneous. It is at least reasonable to ask whether it is lower income inequality on its own that produces the high level of trust, which in turn helps Scandinavian countries suffer less from social problems, or whether their trust levels are a result of some combination of social homogeneity, which makes it easier for people to feel empathy for their fellow citizens, and high levels of education, which gives people a sense that they have the power to shape their own destinies and improve their lives.

There may also be feedback loops between all of these factors. The greater homogeneity of Scandinavian societies may also explain why people are willing to accept much greater levels of income redistribution through the tax and benefit system. If you feel that you are bound to your fellow citizens by common values, culture and heritage, it is likely that you will be willing to do more to provide support to those of them who are worse off than you. And their high levels of education may be a major factor in enabling them to achieve greater income equality, because it equips people in even relatively menial jobs with higher skills and therefore boosts their productivity.

Japan too is a strongly homogeneous society with low levels of immigration and high standards of universal education. So it does not seem fanciful to suggest that it may be these factors that make low income inequality possible. One could imagine them having both a direct impact on trust levels and an indirect one through their effect on income distribution. Japan also has a very particular recent history. One of the reasons Japan has much lower wage differentials between people working at the top and the bottom of private businesses, as well as public sector organisations, is that a revolution that took place in Japanese society after its defeat in the Second World War and swept away the previous class structure and patterns of ownership. In its place, Japan created a new culture, blending modern democratic principles with a traditional subsuming of the interests of the individual in favour of the company, the community and the nation. It is surely naïve to think that we can simply import some of Japan's policies on tax and benefits and achieve the same levels of income inequality and trust in Britain.

It's not as if we haven't tried strongly redistributive policies before. At times in the 1970s, top rates of tax were 83p in the pound on earned income and 98p in the pound on investment income. But, far from producing social harmony based on high levels of trust, it led to economic collapse, driving wealth creators abroad while our biggest businesses were devastated by union militancy. In the last thirteen years, New Labour embarked on a more subtly redistributive programme, which included the minimum wage, higher spending on benefits, generous tax credits and huge increases in spending on public services. But, despite boosting public expenditure by more than half, taking it from 38 per cent to 48 per cent of GDP, New Labour failed to reduce the gap between the rich and the poor. The Gini coefficient – the gap between the richest and the poorest – did decrease between 2000 and 2004, but at the end of the wasted decade it is now at its highest level since 1961.

I am not going to argue that income inequality has nothing to do with the social problems that afflict modern Britain. But I do believe that it is crudely simplistic to reduce complex social issues to a single economic cause. If people do not trust each other in this country, if suspicion and resentment define our attitudes towards our fellow citizens, it is not just because of the widening gap between the richest and poorest. And it will not be reversed by increasing taxes and spending more on benefits, tax credits and public services. Social problems are not all about money. Money alone cannot explain them and money alone cannot cure them. With 'the centre left . . . lost in the cul-de-sac of equality being about money', as James Purnell puts it, it falls to the coalition government to attack the underlying causes of social breakdown, which are rooted in our culture, and relate to the way we raise our families, manage our communities and educate our children.

Tackling low self-esteem and lack of trust

Many of the most disadvantaged people in Britain are denied the support of a strong and loving family, the chance of a good education, close links with neighbours in a well-functioning community and the opportunity to realise their ambitions through gainful employment. I suspect that these contribute at least as much to their anxiety and stress, and any resulting dysfunctional behaviour, as the shortage of money. A glance at the GCSE results of boys on free school meals confirms the importance of family culture and the strength of the communities in which young people are growing up. While 83 per cent from the Chinese community obtained five or more grades A–C, and 64 per cent from Indian communities, white British boys fared worst, with fewer than 40 per cent obtaining these grades. All these young people were from poorer backgrounds, remember, suggesting the importance of factors other than income.

The new government must develop an approach that focuses

on the culture and values that prevail in Britain's poorer families and communities and seeks to shore up positive habits of respect, hard work and mutual support. Forces that threaten to undermine a strong and cohesive culture or that tell people from deprived backgrounds that they are powerless must be resisted and any chances to reinforce an ethos of community solidarity and individual opportunity must be seized. Money will play a part, but only as one of the different ways in which the least well off can be given greater power and control over their lives.

Start young

We should begin at the beginning and focus on the first few years of life, which have such a profound impact on a child's success in adulthood. George Osborne was right to increase the child element of the child tax credit by £150, because lack of money is one of the reasons why some young children are denied the attention of a loving parent or access to books and other things that assist development. I hope that, in future, we can introduce more radical reforms of the child benefits system to increase payments for younger children – either by taxing child benefit for higher rate taxpayers or by reducing the amount of benefit that is paid for older children.

But money alone will not produce strong families or good parents. The coalition already plans to reinvigorate and expand the health visitor service. Health visitors' core role of improving the physical health of both mother and baby, and helping to set up a healthy home environment, remains vital. However, they should also be trained and encouraged to offer support for a wider range of problems facing modern families, such as broken relationships, the involvement of step-parents and a lack of contact with other people in the local community. Health visitors' unique access to people's homes and the strong relationships that they can develop with new parents put them in a perfect situation to introduce parents from challenging circumstances to Sure Start Children's Centres and other support groups and training programmes provided by voluntary organisations, churches and social enterprises. Here they can build networks with other parents and, in time, get advice about how to return to work and organise childcare.

School can change your destiny

We have observed that the countries with the lowest levels of income inequality and the lowest incidence of social problems have strong education systems which seem to achieve good results for the vast majority of their children and not just an elite few. Nothing would do more to give people from poor backgrounds a sense that they have the power to seize the opportunities that life presents than if we could reform our schools so that they serve everyone well and the poorest best of all. But, rather than being engines of social mobility and greater equality, Britain's schools entrench people's inherited advantages and disadvantages. A good education in Britain can be purchased by paying for private schooling, private tuition or moving into a more expensive house in the catchment area of a good state school. Those with fewer resources are often left behind. The system tells them they must take what they are given: there are simply not enough good school places for them to have a meaningful choice. Young people from poor backgrounds are not only deprived of a decent education, but the system also deprives all children the chance to mix with people of different backgrounds. Although this class apartheid diminishes us all and creates a breeding ground for mistrust, it hits the poorest hardest as they lose out on the chance to meet teachers and other students who might encourage them to raise their sights and help them achieve their goals.

Britain's education system will help reduce inequality only when we give those at the bottom of the income scale some of the power that those at the top have. This is the main objective of the reforms that have been announced by the new Education Secretary, Michael Gove, since the election. As Policy Exchange set out in its 2005 report *More Good School Places,* we need to make it easier for new education providers to set up new schools or take over failing ones, so that everyone has a genuine variety to choose from. If, at the same time, we allow teachers to teach and head teachers to do their jobs with less bureaucratic interference, we can expect the simple dynamic of schools competing for pupils to drive up standards in the state sector.

The pupil premium, through which schools will be given additional money for any child from a deprived background, was one of Policy Exchange's key proposals in 2005 and was taken up by both the Conservatives and the Liberal Democrats in their manifestos. It is a vital, and potentially transformative, weapon in the battle against educational inequality, because it will empower disadvantaged children and encourage the best schools to make a special effort to attract those pupils who will benefit most from their teaching. At a time of massive cuts in public spending, it is critically important that we do not allow the pupil premium to become a token payment with no real impact on the education of those who need it most.

Nothing that the new government has done is more important or more inspiring than its programme of radical schools reform. But it needs to go further – to involve all parts of our education system in delivering better schools for more people, to attract private sector energy and capital to the provision of 'free schools', and to entrench the newly granted freedom of independent state schools against subsequent attack by a reactionary educational establishment or a future Labour government.

The last government made a half-hearted attempt to force private schools to do more to justify their charitable status. Many Conservatives opposed this. While it is clear that some Labour ministers were motivated by old-fashioned class envy and spite, it is absolutely right for government to demand a major contribution by private schools to an education strategy that is vital to our national renewal. Private schools must be told that they have a choice. If they want to remain exclusively focused on providing an expensive education to those who can afford it, they should be required to convert into businesses or social enterprises – and pay taxes like any other. If, however, they are willing to play their part in ending education inequalities by setting up new schools in the state system, they will be allowed to retain their privileged tax status. The example of Wellington Academy, sponsored by Wellington College, should become the norm for larger fee-paying schools and the wealthy charitable foundations that own them.

At the same time, the government should allow private companies to set up schools in the state sector and operate them for profit, so long as they accept the conditions applying to all 'free schools' including the admissions policy and the principle of no top-up fees. The British people have long accepted that private companies should be able to make a profit out of supplying healthcare through the NHS, managing prisons, and delivering social care. There is no good reason to deny our education system the benefit of private sector efficiency, innovation and capital – or, rather, to restrict them to the lucky few who can afford to pay private schools' fees. If we are to make the liberalisation of state education truly irreversible, we will need several hundred new 'free schools' to be up and running by the time of the next election. In the current fiscal environment, in which school capital budgets are being cut, this will only happen if the private sector is allowed to play its part and make a reasonable profit doing so.

Having set schools free from bureaucratic control and encouraged parents, teachers, universities, charities and, hopefully, private businesses to set up new schools and take over failing ones, it would be reckless to stand back and let them sink or swim as lone ships on a powerful sea. The educational establishment, who believe in a 'take what you're given' approach to school provision, will regroup. If, as is quite likely, mid-term unpopularity starts costing the Conservatives and Liberal Democrats control of local authorities, Labour-led local education authorities will do everything they can to undermine the freedoms of newly independent academies, and will exploit any pretext to pick off individual schools and force them back under the bureaucratic yoke. If the Labour Party, which is now more in hock to public sector unions than at any time for thirty years, succeed in forming a government again, they will move quickly to renationalise state education and sweep away the liberalising reforms that offer power to parents and teachers and hope to the children who have been failed in recent decades.

The coalition government needs to anticipate the failure of some new academies and put in place rescue procedures to stop such incidents from undermining public trust in the whole reform programme. It needs to work out who will intervene in a failing school that has left local authority control, establish a process for replacing the leadership, transferring the school to an alternative provider or, in extremis, shutting it down and finding alternative schools to offer places to its students. It should have regular conversations with leading providers about schools that are on Ofsted's watch list and do its best to line up a fall-back solution, which can be activated quickly in case of failure.

The government also needs to consolidate the gains made during this legislative session and build institutional and legal fortifications that will render most academies too strong and too popular for a future government to take on. It should set out a vision for an education system in which there are a number of major players competing with each other and smaller, local consortia as well as individual stand-alone schools. Ministers should strongly encourage academies to form chains, through which a number of schools can pool management and administrative overheads and take advantage of one another's specialist teaching or extracurricular resources. They should also require all academies to demonstrate that they have long-term governance plans that will survive the death of any individual or failure of any institution that sponsored them.

National Citizen Service

It is not only in schools that the coalition government should work to boost the self-esteem and confidence of young people and help them understand and trust other people in society. One of the best policies in the coalition programme is the idea of a National Citizen Service for sixteen-year-olds. I was involved in setting up and raising money for last summer's pilot, The Challenge, and have seen the transformative effects of putting a socially mixed group of young people together and challenging them to serve their communities. Young people from tough backgrounds, who were used to feeling like they had been written off, gained self-respect from the realisation that they could achieve something. Those from middle-class backgrounds, especially those who had been privately educated, found their stereotypes challenged and their fear of interaction with other young people greatly reduced. Rolling this policy out nationally will be expensive and should, in any event, be done slowly and carefully. But I fervently believe that National Citizen Service has a crucial role to play in increasing the levels of trust in our society and mitigating the dysfunctional behaviour that blights so many lives in Britain.

Work is the best therapy

One of the biggest contributors to income inequality in modern Britain is the endemic worklessness that exists in millions of British households. The people affected are separated from the rest of society by a gulf; resentment and distrust grows on both sides. Supporting people with benefits when they suffer misfortune is an essential feature of a civilised society. But Britain's welfare state entrenches inequality by making it less onerous, and more profitable, for millions of people to subsist on benefits than go out and get a job. In a recent poll conducted by the Centre for

Social Justice, only 25 per cent of benefit claimants thought that they would be better off from working, with 39 per cent feeling that they would be worse off if they worked more. As a result, government statistics tell us that there are 4.8 million working-age people in households in which nobody works, 1.5 million people on jobseeker's allowance, almost five million out-of-work benefit claimants, and 1.4 million under-25s who are neither working nor in full-time education. This is not merely a result of the recession: 1.4 million people in the UK have been on out-of-work benefits for nine or more of the last ten years.

Being out of work for long periods saps the spirit and deprives people of contact with the rest of society, exacerbating the anxiety and mistrust that Richard Wilkinson and Kate Pickett pinpoint as the causes of dysfunctional behaviour. The answer is not to transfer more income to people subsisting on benefits, as this will simply exacerbate the division of our society into two mutually hostile camps of those who work and those who don't. Instead we must reform the benefits system so that it helps prepare people for work and provides incentives for people to get off welfare and stand on their own two feet.

Immigration

The urgent need to get British people back into work means that we also need to limit unskilled immigration, as I discussed in the previous chapter. The massive influx of unskilled workers in the last thirteen years may have benefited British businesses and their customers – but, according to the OECD, it meant that more than 70 per cent of new jobs went to workers born overseas and suppressed the wages paid for low-skilled jobs, making it even less attractive for British citizens to move off benefits and back into work.

Home is where the heart is

Housing is another area in which the poorer members of our society are disempowered and excluded. Where we live helps to form our sense of self, who we mix with and how we imagine our futures. Creating strong communities in which people from all walks of life live together is an essential step in building a more harmonious and cohesive society. The dream of owning a home remains just that for many at the bottom, with the average home costing over £220,000 in the first quarter of 2010. Despite a fall in prices over the recession, the overall trend remains for prices to outpace incomes, making home ownership more difficult. Prices rose by 273 per cent in real terms between 1959 and 2009, compared to real earnings growth of 169 per cent. The main reason for this is that Britain's planning system has been paralysed by a Mexican stand-off between a Labour government that has imposed crude housing targets from the centre and local communities which, in the absence of proper financial incentives to allow new houses to be built, have refused to do so. As a result, an estimated 156,816 houses were built in 2009, compared to 425,800 in 1968. The prospect of owning their own home is becoming a distant chimera for increasing numbers of young families, who are encouraged to share this peculiarly British dream and then find themselves shut out of it.

Social housing plays an even bigger part in the splintering

of our society into mutually distrustful ghettos, rich and poor. The post-war slum clearance and rehousing programmes broke up established communities and put people into what George Orwell called 'monstrously inhuman' and 'soulless' estates, far from their roots and separate from other social classes. Over several decades, many of these estates turned into social swamps breeding crime, addiction and family breakdown. The effect of large-scale immigration exacerbated the problem in some places. In *The New East End*, Geoff Dench, Kate Gavron and Michael Young anatomised the sense of betrayal felt by members of the white working class who were excluded from their own communities as

> the welfare state . . . turned . . . from a mutual-aid society writ
> large . . . into a complex, centralised and bureaucratic system run
> by middle-class do-gooders who gave generously to those who
> put nothing into the pot while making ordinary working people
> who did contribute feel like recipients of charity when drawing
> their own entitlements.

The main problem with the current system of social housing is its inflexibility – the way that the principle of lifetime tenure interacts with the scarce supply of social housing to make people reluctant to leave a council or housing association flat or house. This then narrows their horizons, acts as a brake on their ambition and defines them as a permanent member of a separate, subsidised, class. Social housing should be a transitional solution for younger families getting started in life and for people who face temporary hardship or misfortune and need the protection of subsidised housing while they get back on their feet. Only older people who have not been able to save enough to buy their own home should view it as a final destination, which they can rely on until they die.

While some council housing estates have become dystopian worlds unto themselves, Britain has also seen the growth in gated communities, in which the fearful middle classes attempt to pull up the drawbridge and protect themselves from those of lesser means. While those who have been traumatised by persistent burglaries and terrorised by yobs deserve both sympathy and effective neighbourhood policing, gated communities are not an answer to any social ill. They will only accelerate the fragmentation of our society into separate tribes and pour petrol on the flames of conflict between them.

The errors of post-war housing and planning policies will not be undone overnight, but the coalition government has set out good plans to start tackling them, inspired by the research conducted by Alan Evans and Oliver Hartwich for Policy Exchange. The introduction of a new homes bonus, which enables local authorities to retain six years' worth of the council tax attached to any additional house (without losing the equivalent amount in central government grant), is particularly important. But, in the long run, it would be much simpler and more powerful to reduce central government's role in funding local services and to free councils to raise a range of local taxes, so that people recognise that there is an iron link between local development (whether of additional houses or of new business premises) and revenue for community infrastructure and services.

The government should also press on with reforms to social housing tenure. Expansion of mixed-ownership schemes and the introduction of a right for social tenants to exchange a property in one place for an equivalent property elsewhere in the country are good initiatives. But, over the next ten years, the government should seek to limit the tenure for all new tenants – and to incentivise current tenants of working age to accept new tenancies with five-year term limits. In this way, a limited stock of social housing will be able to support a much larger number of people navigating a phase of greater need, rather than hold a small number of people forever captive in a social cul-de-sac.

Although some people in Britain are persuaded that 'good fences make good neighbours', the government should assert that there is no substitute for the mutual understanding and respect that stems from constant conversation and interaction. One of the small number of nationally determined planning policies that should survive the coalition government's decentralising planning reforms is a ban on new gated communities or any extensions to existing ones, so we don't allow new walls to divide us.

New forms of social glue

Enlightened housing policies will help us restore a society in which the poor do not inhabit a totally different world to the rest. But modern Britain is so polarised that bridging the two nations will require new institutions and habits of behaviour to reconnect them. The charities, clubs and associations that bring people together have been squeezed out by a range of economic and social forces, including the structure of the welfare state, which has often replaced them in the delivery of local services. In the past, churches, trade unions, credit unions and friendly societies were dignified institutions that commanded respect in deprived communities and set an example of good behaviour for people to follow. None of these institutions are as strong as they once were. When people need help, they are encouraged to look upwards to remote and impersonal branches of the central state, not around to their own home-grown networks of mutual support. When they fall into drugs and petty crime, there is no channel for the community to express its disapproval, only the unlikely possibility of a police arrest, and there is no form of sanction that the community can impose, only the distant prospect of a prison sentence, which will destroy the individual's few remaining ties to the community that could give them roots.

Renewing the glue that binds communities together and makes our society strong is a vastly ambitious enterprise and government's power to bring it about is limited. But it does have a role. When commissioning services, all bits of government, whether central or local, should ask if they can construct a patchwork quilt of charities, voluntary groups, churches and local businesses to deliver what people need, rather than impose the suffocating blanket of monopoly provision by a state agency or national contractor. Giving local people more control over how their communities are policed and how their local park is maintained should help to create more active neighbours, benign busybodies working for the good of their local area. While cuts in public spending will inflict pain on all sectors of society, and particularly on those who rely on public services most, the unavoidable constraints imposed by the fiscal crisis should force central and local government bureaucrats to relax their grip on decision-making and allow a vibrant cacophony of new voices to shape debate about what is best for our communities. Although the process will probably be chaotic and may sometimes fail, the involvement of people in thousands of different conversations around the country, spanning age groups and races and classes, will do more to cure Britain's social ills than any increase in spending on benefits for the poor.

Big Society, not redistributive state

Modern Conservatives share with their Liberal Democrat colleagues a genuine disquiet at rising inequality and a solemn determination that the coalition government's most important mission is to improve the lives of the least well off. But we do not believe that getting the state to intervene more to redistribute income and wealth from the rich to poor will produce that result. If we can give the poorest children in the country the chance to attend really good schools, if we can break down the physical and social barriers that divide communities, if we can help everyone recognise that work is the quickest way to build self-esteem, if we can give people the power and resources to come together to solve local problems, then a happier, healthier, more trusting Britain will be our reward. That is the Big Society that Liberal Democrats and Conservatives want to create.

5. Managing migration to keep our kingdom united

I have changed my mind about immigration. I grew up during the 1970s in a small village in the Berkshire countryside, where there was little evidence of mass immigration. After university, I spent a couple of years living in the United States, a country created by mass immigration and defined by the romantic story of an American dream available, at least in theory, to anyone willing to pledge allegiance to the Stars and Stripes. For most of the last twenty years, I have lived a metropolitan life in the centre of London. There, I was the unthinking beneficiary of large-scale immigration – I partied with people from every corner of the globe, ate out in restaurants serving every culture's best cooking and enjoyed myself in cafes, bars and shops staffed by motivated and hard-working young people from all over the planet. Mass immigration made my life more fun, my diet more spicy and my money go further. It was easy to take a relaxed view of immigration and denigrate those who sounded the alarm about its scale and impact as closet racists and little Englanders.

It was only when I was elected onto Westminster City Council that I began to discover the downside of mass immigration. As chairman of the housing committee, I had to help the council wrestle with the pressure on social housing from asylum seekers and other migrants. It made it impossible for young adult children to find accommodation in the communities in which they had grown up and where their parents still lived. It imposed huge costs on local taxpayers and it consigned families of asylum seekers to spend months, sometimes years, in totally inappropriate bed and breakfast accommodation, unable to work legally or to become part of any community.

My doubts grew when I read *The New East End* by Geoff Dench, Kate Gavron and Michael Young. The authors' brilliant study of population flows and housing occupancy in east London painted a devastating portrait of well-functioning, if impoverished, communities, being displaced by new waves of immigration. Their account was all the more powerful because they clearly took no pleasure in analysing the negative effects of mass immigration into the East End and evinced nothing but sympathy for the plight of the immigrants themselves, who were, after all, doing nothing more criminal than trying to make a better life for themselves and their children.

Then came the 7 July bombings in London. As we learned more about the bombers, we discovered that they had been born in Britain, gone to local schools, played cricket at local clubs; one had even become a primary school teacher. Something had clearly gone very wrong in the communities in which these young men grew up. While nothing diminishes the bombers' personal responsibility for their evil acts, it was plain that, for decades, we had failed to integrate recent immigrants into our society or pass on our values to them and their children. What measures existed to help immigrants become British had been overwhelmed by the sheer scale of the immigration flows and the authorities' total loss of control over who was coming into the country and where they were settling.

Now we face a fiscal crisis which will require drastic cuts in public spending. We will not be able to sustain a social contract in which schooling and healthcare are provided to all citizens free of charge and are funded by taxation if we continue to allow, every year, hundreds of thousands of people from around the world to join the queues at A&E and send their children to British schools. Nor can we sit back while eight million British citizens of working age either shun or are shut out from all forms of useful economic activity because employers can find migrant workers who will accept subsistence wages to do menial jobs.

A new immigration settlement

Britain needs a new immigration settlement, involving tighter controls on the number of people who can move into the UK every year (from both inside and outside the EU), greater selectiveness about who is allowed to settle here, tougher financial demands on new immigrants and those who want to employ them, more robust measures to remove those who break our laws, and more intensive efforts to ensure that all those who do settle in Britain adopt British values and become part of a truly united kingdom.

The last government started to introduce tighter controls on the number of people who can move into the UK from outside the EU. The adoption of a system under which would-be immigrants are awarded points for different qualifications and only those with a minimum level of points are considered for work permits is a welcome start. The next step is for the coalition government to set an upper limit on the total amount of net migration into the UK from outside the EU. Britain's ageing population and lack of skills in certain sectors mean that we will almost certainly need to have some net immigration. But it should probably be of the order of 20,000–50,000 a year.

Surety deposit

A reduction in the number of new immigrants from outside the EU will go some way to restraining the pressure on public services. But we also need to tackle the legitimate sense, which some hard-pressed taxpayers have, that they are being taken for a ride by people who come to Britain in order to take advantage of its free schooling and healthcare. It is vitally important to most British people's sense of fairness that essential public services like schooling and healthcare are universally available and free to all. It would not be right to introduce specific user charges for those who have recently settled in the country – all our efforts should be to make recent immigrants feel part of our society, not to emphasise their separateness. But that does not mean that it is unreasonable or impossible to ask new migrants from outside the EU to make a financial commitment to the UK, in exchange for the protection of its laws and the benefits of its public services.

It would go a long way to satisfy the essentially fair-minded British people that their generosity was not being abused, if any non-EU migrant seeking leave to remain in the UK for more than a short stay were required to deposit funds with Her Majesty's Government as surety for their good behaviour and commitment not to exploit British hospitality. The government would repay the deposit once the individual had paid income tax for a specified number of years or an amount equivalent to several times the value of the deposit. But it would be forfeited if the individual were convicted of any offence or had lived here for more than, say, three years, without contributing to the Exchequer through income tax.

The level of the deposit could be varied for different categories of non-EU migrant. The government could decide to offer discounts for immigrants with particular skills, if it judged that it was in the national interest to bring them to Britain, and employers could be encouraged to finance the deposits of immigrants whose employment would benefit their businesses. Would-be immigrants around the world would be able to check on the level of deposit required, which would be set once a year, and would be able to make arrangements to borrow the money from extended families and local financial intermediaries, once they had amassed sufficient points to qualify for a visa.

A system of this kind has the potential to transform relations between existing British residents and those who migrate to our shores. Indigenous and long-established British citizens would be reassured that recent migrants are paying their way and are not taking the rest of us for a ride. Recent immigrants would gain confidence from the knowledge that each of them has done their bit to contribute to the public purse and that they have as much of a right to claim the protection of our laws and the benefit of our public services as anyone whose ancestors arrived with Julius Caesar or William the Conqueror.

Students

While it is strongly in the national interest to reduce the number of people from outside the EU who move to Britain each year to live and work, it would be deeply damaging to Britain's future prosperity for restrictions to be placed on the number of young people who come here to study. In its attempt to clamp down on the abuse of the student visa system by economic migrants, the UK Border Agency has introduced new rules that make it almost impossible for young foreigners to get the general student visas that enable them to study at English language schools and work for up to ten hours a week to help pay for the cost of being here. This is a mistake. The government needs to deter unskilled immigrants from using rogue colleges to cheat the system, not put off the genuine students who want to learn our language and form a relationship with our country.

EU controls

Anyone who was a candidate for one of the three main parties at this year's general election will have sensed our common failure to address the elephant in the room of the immigration debate, which is the level of immigration from eastern Europe. While Conservatives were able to promise a cap on immigration from outside the EU, all we were able to say about immigration from other EU member states was that Tony Blair should have taken the opportunity to introduce transitional controls on immigration from eastern Europe, when Poland and others joined the EU, and that we will introduce such controls on immigration from any new member states that join the EU in future. Although it had the merit of honesty, it was clear to everyone that this was a policy to shut the stable door long after the horse had bolted.

The UK should seek to impose permanent restrictions on the free flow of people from any new member states, such as Croatia or Turkey, but the retrospective introduction of controls on immigration from existing EU member states would be hugely controversial and very unlikely to be accepted by other EU countries. Nevertheless, there are other steps the coalition government could take which would help allay public concern about immigration from within the EU.

I am the MP for the south-western corner of Lincolnshire, a county which has seen large numbers of migrant workers from eastern Europe come in to work in the fields harvesting vegetables. When I talked to people about immigration during the election campaign, I soon discovered that most of them had a high respect for the work ethic of Polish migrants in particular. What caused anger and resentment was the sense that some EU migrants were abusing our benefits system, by claiming child benefit for children not even living in the UK, putting unreasonable pressure on the NHS by travelling to the UK to give birth or get treatment for long-term conditions, or jumping the queue for scarce social housing. If the coalition government were seen to take robust action to tackle some of these abuses, even at the risk of legal challenge, I believe it would do a great deal to reassure people that Britain is not letting its generosity be exploited.

How can this be done? European Directive 2004/38/EC deals with the right of the citizens of the Union and their family members to move freely within the territory of the member states and live where they like. This directive maintains the requirement that EU citizens need to 'exercise an economic activity or dispose of sufficient resources in order to take up residence in another Member State'. If this requirement was incorporated into British law, it should now be robustly enforced. If it wasn't properly incorporated, the relevant legislation should be amended to give the authorities the power to do so. In future, whenever a migrant from within the EU applies to a central or local government authority for benefits or housing or part of the NHS for non-emergency healthcare, that authority should be required to check whether the individual in question either has a job or sufficient funds to support themselves in the UK. If they don't, they should be told to leave the country and be denied all benefits and other services (except emergency healthcare) on the basis that they are not legally resident in the UK.

It should also be possible to challenge some other alleged abuses. EU social security co-ordination rules make clear that, in the event that one parent is resident in the UK but the children are resident in another EU member state, any family benefits that are based on residence (such as child benefit) should be paid by the country where the children are living, not the UK. EU migrants claiming child benefit in the UK should be required to provide evidence that their children are resident in the UK and this should be checked on a regular basis. This approach should be firmly enforced and defended in the courts, if necessary.

The government should also act to exclude recent migrants from EU member states from waiting lists for social housing. Social housing is in scarce supply and should be reserved for long-standing residents with real need. We should pass legislation to restrict social housing to people who have been resident in the UK for at least five years, so that the right to social housing becomes something that you earn after a sustained commitment to British society.

Language and history

Tighter rules on immigration will not automatically restore the sense that we are all part of one nation, of a truly united kingdom. To do this, we need to take a much more robust approach to ensuring that immigrants to Britain understand our culture, adopt our values and, in time, become British.

In the years following the 7 July bombings in London, Labour ministers made dozens of speeches and launched countless initiatives to celebrate Britishness, define British values, articulate a national mission statement and coin a national motto. These essentially flawed efforts were the product of a simplistic interpretation of American and French political history and every liberal intellectual's envy for the constitutional clarity provided by a successful revolution.

Searching for a simple expression of our national idea – something like '*liberté, égalité, fraternité*' or 'government by the people, for the people, of the people' – is destined to fail because it misses the point. Equally misconceived is the attempt to define a set of essential British values, which always seems to end up with a banal recitation of general human virtues such as tolerance and fair play. It is not a matter of chance that Britain has no written constitution. Britain's constitutional arrangements have evolved in a haphazard, piecemeal and organic way. They do not form part of a rational scheme – they are more like an ecosystem than a piece of engineering.

To get to the root of what it means to be British, you need to go to the fundamental facts that make Britain unique among nations. The first, and most important, fact about Britain is that it is the birthplace of the English language. English is Britain's greatest achievement, its most remarkable invention, its finest work of art. Like Britain's democratic institutions, the English language is constantly evolving but never loses the thread connecting it to the words and phrases of Chaucer and Shakespeare and the King James Bible. So when someone settles in Britain, we need to make it an absolute requirement that they learn our language. This should involve an end to the translation of official documents and websites into foreign languages and the provision of interpreters at public expense – and the diversion of the money saved into subsidies for English language courses in adult education colleges, Jobcentres, churches, mosques and community centres.

The genius of English is that, once they have mastered it, immigrants can make it their own. The arrival and integration of new groups of settlers has always ended up contributing to the further evolution of our language. As a newcomer to Britain, you know that you really belong when you hear someone of completely different background using words that you and your compatriots have introduced to the language. That moment arrived long ago for the Huguenots and the Jews, more recently for settlers from the West Indies, Bangladesh and Pakistan. When we hear Polish jokes and Somali swearwords on the late night comedy shows and at the back of the school bus, we know that they too will have been fully woven in to the rich cloth of British identity.

The second most important fact about Britain is its age. It is made up of nations that have existed for centuries. Anyone who grows up in Britain is surrounded by the physical evidence of that history in churches, cottages, grand country houses, garden squares, town halls. Even if you live and work in a wholly twentieth-century city like Milton Keynes, British newspapers, magazines and TV programmes are full of images of our ancient past. It is impossible to have a deep feeling of connection to Britain, or any understanding of our democratic institutions, if you don't know the broad shape of its history and appreciate its Thames-like meandering flow. Magna Carta, the Gunpowder Plot, the Civil War, the Restoration, the Great Reform Acts, the Beveridge Report – these are the volcanic events that created Britain's democratic landscape. The coalition government should insist that the epic narrative of British history is taught in all primary and secondary schools to all schoolchildren, and given particular attention in schools where there are large numbers of pupils whose parents settled here.

Once newcomers to Britain have learned English and studied our history, they will be able to fit into British society, laugh at British jokes and appreciate the strength and durability of our institutions – Parliament, the monarchy, the judiciary and the armed forces – and their centuries-long success in keeping Britain prosperous, safe and free.

Asserting belonging

The process of assimilating and integrating new migrants is a crucial first step to restoring a sense of one nation. But the 7 July bombings demonstrate that it can take time for a sense of alienation in migrant communities to manifest itself. People who themselves took the initiative to move to Britain are often more willing to integrate than their children, who were born in Britain but may encounter racism while growing up, and can become confused by the apparent clash between the inherited values of their families' religion or culture and the acquired values of modern, secular Britain. Even if future levels of net migration are restrained by some of the policies outlined above, there is still much to do to help the children of everyone who has made their home here in the last forty years feel bound to their compatriots by common values, a shared culture and mutual respect and understanding.

The process needs to start when children first go to school. One of the ways in which the United States has achieved a remarkable level of assimilation and integration, despite constant flows of new migrants from a kaleidoscope of countries, is by establishing the convention that all public schools begin the school day with a recitation of the pledge of allegiance. 'I pledge allegiance to the flag of the United States of America, and to the republic for which it stands, one nation under God, indivisible, with liberty and justice for all,' they intone.

It is time to introduce a similar ceremony in British schools. While the precise wording of the pledge should be left to better writers and philosophers than me, I think we need something more than the oath of allegiance required of members of Parliament and other officeholders, which requires allegiance only to the monarch and her successors. Instead, it should make brief reference to the essential institutions to which we wish all British children to develop an instinctive loyalty (the monarchy, the union and Parliament) as well as vital concepts such as freedom and the rule of law. Children in Scotland, Wales and Northern Ireland could recite a slightly different pledge, referring to their own nation and its democratic institutions.

Recitation of the pledge would not be compulsory – that would be offensive to the freedom of speech that is one of the hallmarks of our democracy. But it would not need to be. If it were introduced in the first year of primary school and established as a daily convention to which most children and teachers adhered, then it would generate its own gravitational pull. In later years, when older children see a refusal to take part as a pleasing act of rebellion, the social norm would be established, its power asserted by the very fact that it triggers teenage revolt.

A new form of National Service

While many contemporary policy wonks would appear to agree with the Jesuits - 'give me the boy until he is seven and I will show you the man' – the transition from childhood to adulthood presents another opportunity to cement a sense of shared values and common purpose in Britain's hugely diverse population. In the months that followed the 7 July bombings, during his campaign for the Conservative leadership, David Cameron proposed the establishment of a national scheme of service in which young people of all backgrounds would be brought together in teams, set testing challenges that help them develop as young adults and put to work on projects benefiting the wider community. His ambition was for National Citizen Service to become a universal rite of passage, which would mark the start of adulthood, break down barriers between classes, races and creeds and instil at an early age an understanding of the communities in which we live and a commitment to helping others less fortunate than ourselves.

As head of the Conservative Party's implementation team for the two years leading up to the election, one of my responsibilities was to work with a small start-up charity called The Challenge to turn Cameron's ideas about National Citizen Service into reality and create a working model of a programme for young people who have just completed their GCSEs. The coalition agreement envisages the gradual roll-out of National Citizen Service for young people based on the model developed by The Challenge and Cameron recently announced that the government would pay for 10,000 young people to do National Citizen Service in 2011. Nothing would do more to bring the diverse communities of Britain together than if, by 2020, every teenager were taking part in National Citizen Service as a matter of course.

Defending our values

As well as implementing policies to instil our values in all young people growing up here, the government needs to be robust in defending British society against those who would take advantage of our freedoms to infiltrate our institutions and attack us from within. Policy Exchange and others have published reports revealing the promotion of extreme Islamist ideas in some British mosques, universities and colleges. Policy Exchange also published Martin Bright's exposure of a culture of appeasement among some senior civil servants responsible for the government's work on both counter-terrorism and social cohesion. Their argument seems to be that because some Islamic extremists have been critical of al-Qaeda, they represent potential allies in an attempt to turn disaffected young British Muslims away from terrorism and it therefore makes sense for the British government to turn a blind eye to their extreme ideas. Recently it was revealed that Home Office civil servants in the

Office of Security and Counter-Terrorism had publicly criticised Theresa May's decision to refuse a visa to the Islamist preacher Zakir Naik. This is intolerable.

We cannot defend the liberal values that Britain has done so much to bring into being if we compromise with those who want to eradicate them. We will not persuade the next generation of Muslim leaders to promote a modern, ecumenical interpretation of Islam that can co-exist peacefully with people of other religions and none if we ignore the intolerance of some of the worst demagogues defiling the daily prayers of the devout. A coalition government that has put the first Muslim woman into a British cabinet and draws on the best of the liberal tradition must challenge extremists, whether they masquerade as patriots in the BNP or as preachers in the service of Allah.

One Nation

Some of the proposals in this chapter are unashamedly conservative and may trouble some Liberal Democrats. But we all want Britain to be one nation and everyone in it to feel a genuine sense of loyalty to the country, solidarity with their fellow citizens and pride in our liberal values. One of the most striking features of the last general election campaign was the detachment of the political classes from some of the deepest concerns of the British people and the anger this fuelled. Nowhere was this more stark than in relation to the Labour government's refusal to address the growing resentment caused by more than a decade of mass immigration. Gordon Brown's scathing words about Mrs Gillian Duffy were so important because they revealed the gulf that had opened up between rulers and ruled. Nothing would do more to undermine public confidence in the coalition than if it compounded Labour's failure and ducked the difficult decisions needed to keep Britain united and at peace.

6. Securing our energy supplies and saving the climate

There is no area of government responsibility in which Britain has suffered more from Labour's decade of indecisiveness than in energy policy. It has been clear for a long time that the closure of Britain's coal-fired power plants and the decommissioning of our ageing nuclear power stations would withdraw a substantial proportion of our electricity-generating capacity by the end of this decade. It has also been clear that our North Sea oil and gas reserves were coming to an end and that we would become increasingly dependent on imports of fossil fuels from unstable and potentially hostile parts of the world such as the Middle East, north Africa and Russia. But instead of acting early to diversify our sources of supply and bring alternative generating capacity on stream, the last government buried its head in the sand. Labour ministers spent the best part of a decade ducking all the difficult decisions and trusting that vague aspirations about onshore wind farms and greater energy efficiency would somehow fill the gap. As a direct result, Britain faces a real possibility of power cuts and price spikes, not to mention an increase in our carbon emissions as carbon-free nuclear generation is shut down.

While the looming threats to Britain's energy security were largely ignored, Labour politicians focused most of their attention on climate change. But what characterised their approach was an extraordinary, and very damaging, disparity between the rhetoric about climate change, which was emotional and relentless, and government action to cut our carbon emissions, which was piecemeal, tardy and confused. The Labour government swallowed without question every hypothesis advanced by climate scientists. They went along with even the most alarmist claims, maybe because they thought that it might help shock the British people out of their complacency and build support for painful sacrifices to come. No global talking shop was complete without one of the Miliband brothers, earnestly urging the United States or China to repent and bow before that shiny new suit of imperial vestments, the global target for emissions cuts.

But what did they actually achieve? At last year's disastrous Copenhagen conference, far from leading the world, Britain ended up cheerleading for a half-baked fudge that had been cooked up in our absence by four large developing countries and the US. Back home, the actions of Labour ministers fell woefully short of the hype and consisted of a blizzard of initiatives, too small and too numerous to have any consistent, long-term impact on investors' decisions and individuals' behaviour. As a result, Britain's reliance on fossil fuels actually increased in the decade from 1998 to 2008.

The coalition government needs to be much more hard headed in its approach to the twin threats to Britain's energy security and the world's climate. Ministers should distinguish between facts and theories, conduct unsentimental analysis of the risks of different outcomes and design a small number of practical policies to deliver new, diversified, low-carbon energy infrastructure. Most important of all, they should then stick to them.

First, the facts. As much as half of Britain's current electricity-generating fleet is forecast to be shut down between now and 2020, as old plants reach the end of their life and the EU's Large Combustion Plant Directive forces dirtier plants to close. If we do nothing, it won't be long before our lights start going out. Meanwhile, the result of Britain's 'dash for gas' in the 1990s is that 40 per cent of this country's electricity production now comes from gas. This has left us increasingly exposed to imports as our North Sea reserves continue to decline. More than 70 per cent of Britain's primary energy supply will come from imports by 2020 if current trends continue. While natural gas supplies have become more plentiful in recent years, it would not take much to put Britain's neck under the Russians' boots. The Ukrainians will tell us that this is not a comfortable place to be.

Now, the theories. Like all scientific hypotheses, climate change science deals with probabilities rather than certainties. There appears to be strong evidence for an increase in average global temperatures since the start of industrialisation in the West. Each of the logical steps in the argument that there is a link between rising levels of carbon dioxide (CO_2) in the upper atmosphere and rising temperatures seems reasonable. But the extrapolation of future temperature changes from current and predicted levels of CO_2 emissions remains uncertain, not least because of feedback loops that could reinforce the greenhouse effect.

Climate change scientists have tended to describe their findings in absolute terms and have been excessively intolerant of dissent. Politicians and campaigners have been especially irresponsible, reaching for apocalyptic language and images to attract public attention, and then suffering a massive loss of credibility when some of their more lurid claims were shown to be based on fundamental errors. But, despite the exaggeration and the mistakes, the evidence that human activity is causing the global climate to warm and that further warming could result in abrupt changes to atmospheric and oceanic systems is overwhelming.

Climate change could affect the United Kingdom directly. Rising sea levels would lead to more frequent flooding in low-lying areas, for example in the east and south-east. Although the UK, as a rich, temperate country, would be relatively well placed to adapt to any large climatic changes, many other countries would not be so fortunate. Climate change would be likely to lead to a greater number of conflicts over resources, to more failed states and to greater migration pressures. These trends would threaten Britain's national security.

Just as individuals routinely take out insurance policies against uncertain and imprecisely known future risks, it is prudent for countries to take out an insurance policy against the risks posed by climate change, by reducing the greenhouse gas emissions normally associated with modern life and helping vulnerable parts of the world adapt to a hotter climate. The costs of such action, while large, should be easily affordable: in the order of a few per cent of global GDP, if not lower, according to the most credible economic studies. Electricity prices will need to increase by around 10 per cent or more by 2020 to fund greater quantities of low-carbon energy, according to a recent study by the European Climate Foundation. But that would be far less than the increase in energy prices that occurred in the past decade as a result of higher fossil fuel costs. In fact, one of the attractions of low carbon energy is that prices, while higher on average, tend to be much more stable than those of fossil fuels.

As well as the need to insure against risks to our future wellbeing, there is also the potential for the UK to benefit from international action to ward off climate change. Moves to reduce energy consumption and increase the production of low-carbon energy are gathering pace around the world. More than 700 policies to cut carbon and boost renewable energy have been introduced by national, local and regional governments over the past decade. The growing global market for goods and services related to low-carbon energy represents a huge economic opportunity, which the UK should embrace.

Other countries' experience suggests that the best way to build competitive low-carbon industries, and create associated jobs, is to stimulate those industries in which you have a natural competitive advantage at home. Denmark was of the first countries to promote wind energy and is now home to a number of leading global wind equipment exporters such as Vestas. China is exploiting its comparative advantage in low-cost manufacturing to take a global lead in solar panel production with flagship companies including Yingli Solar.

Britain's approach to climate change and energy security should be based on a clear-eyed view of her strengths and weaknesses and a ruthless focus on our national interest. It should comprise a new energy strategy, a new carbon tax, other measures to encourage low carbon living and a new approach to international diplomacy.

Energy strategy

After a decade of dither and drift, Britain does not have the luxury of being able to keep the lights on, reduce its dependence on imports of foreign energy supplies and dramatically cut carbon emissions all at the same time. We need to prioritise – and accept that some goals will take longer to achieve than others, that some may even cut across one another in the short and medium term. Balancing the trade-offs with the opportunities, Britain should look to gas and nuclear power plants to fulfil an increasingly important role in meeting our electricity needs for the next ten years, while singling out offshore renewables for long-term development into a major component of our energy supply, in the hope that they can take the strain and reduce our reliance on imported gas in the more distant future.

Nuclear power, the main alternative to coal for providing stable base-load power generation, offers greater energy security and a way to reduce the risk of damaging changes in the climate. It uses uranium, a ubiquitous feedstock compared with scarce and concentrated fossil fuels, and has very low CO_2 emissions. The coalition government's energy strategy must make the promotion of nuclear power one of its top priorities. The first step must be to ensure that the existing nuclear capacity is replaced. This will require a government-led national strategy for the disposal, reprocessing and storage of nuclear waste. If we are to have any chance of increasing nuclear capacity above current levels, we will also need to do more to reassure local people about the safety of nuclear plants and create a clear and predictable system of incentives for communities that embrace them. Improved public education, particularly on the issue of nuclear waste, will also be critical: it's estimated that if an individual's lifetime electricity needs were supplied entirely by nuclear power, the resulting waste would fill a Coke can, with close to zero carbon emissions, while the equivalent waste from coal generation would be more than 60 tons of solid waste and 70 tons of CO_2.

Leading nuclear power developers, such as EDF, have made it clear that they do not need subsidies to build new nuclear plants. But nuclear power stations demand a very large upfront investment – with the initial capital outlay paid back slowly, over decades – so greater clarity, certainty and stability in the long-term price of carbon is essential. This is one of the key reasons why Britain should introduce a carbon tax (as I set out below).

The coalition government's energy strategy should also recognise the unacceptable environmental damage caused by burning coal without carbon capture and storage (CCS) and look to phase out coal-fired plants over the next twenty years by allowing them to be retired as they age, fail to meet pollution regulations or become economically unviable due to carbon pricing. The last government made lots of noise about developing CCS technology in the UK, so that 'clean coal' might become part of our long-term energy mix, but it ended up delivering nothing. As CCS involves a collection of technologies that is as yet unproven on a commercial scale and which is likely to cost at least £500 million per plant, it would be folly to spend vast amounts of public money on developing such a plant in Britain. CCS is more likely to be deployed initially in large industrialising countries like India and China, where a large number of new coal power stations are needed in the coming years and where it is easier to push through multi-billion-pound strategic infrastructure projects. If they succeed in bringing the costs of the technology down, the

British government can always revisit the question of clean coal in the future.

Building new gas-fired power plants involves difficult trade-offs between two important priorities: boosting our energy security and cutting carbon emissions. Natural gas emits about half as much carbon as coal so it will help us achieve our climate objectives if it replaces coal generation. But building more gas plants would increase our reliance on imports. Unfortunately we have no choice, if we want to keep Britain's lights on and factories humming. We must build more gas plants. In the meantime, we can improve our energy security by implementing several complementary policies. Increasing Britain's meagre gas storage capacity would make this country less vulnerable to sudden supply disruptions. Reintroducing capacity guarantees – incentives for the market to build surplus gas infrastructure and back-up power capacity – would also help protect us against supply shocks. Another way to enhance security would be by building bigger and better facilities for the import and transportation of liquefied natural gas (LNG), as this would give us the option to source gas from different parts of the world. Thanks to massive investment in LNG infrastructure over the past few years, Cambridge Energy Research Associates estimates the UK could now source up to 40 per cent of its gas needs from the world's eighteen exporters of LNG, compared with just 1 per cent in 2005. And it is possible that new sources of unconventional gas could be found in the coming years within the EU – as happened in the United States, where a quiet revolution in shale gas production over the past decade has made the country self-sufficient in natural gas.

The ineffectiveness of Labour's tinkering with energy policy is thrown into sharp relief by an assessment of Britain's progress in expanding the production of renewable energy. Despite the last government's inflated climate change rhetoric, in the EU only Malta and Luxembourg have a lower percentage of renewables in their energy mix than Britain, according to a recent European Commission report. The most important lesson for the coalition to learn is the importance of identifying one or two sectors where Britain has an innate competitive advantage, and giving them significant and consistent support. Instead of playing around with onshore wind farms one week, solar energy the next and CCS the week after that, Britain should focus on her advantages as an island. This country has among the world's best offshore wind, wave and tidal resources: large amounts of wind from the Atlantic Ocean, significant tidal ranges, and large quantities of shallow water close to the major centres of energy demand. We also possess world-beating offshore marine engineering skills as a legacy from the North Sea oil and gas industry, and many of the businesses in this sector are seeking alternative markets for their equipment and know-how.

Even if the government does introduce a carbon tax, as I propose, the market alone is unlikely to be able to mobilise the more than £100 billion of capital estimated to be needed for the UK to meet its 2020 renewable energy targets. Significant government intervention will be needed. This support should be in the form of muscular yet targeted government interventions. Rather than starting with economics textbooks – like the designers of the complex, ineffective and expensive Renewables Obligation, which places an onus on UK electricity suppliers to source an increasing proportion of their electricity from renewable sources – we should start with what works in the real world. Brazil has created a sugarcane ethanol industry from scratch over the past thirty years and brought it to a point where it now supplies more than half of the country's fuel needs using less than 1 per cent of its land. The key to its success has been a clear, simple and consistent biofuels-blending mandate imposed on fuel suppliers, combined with government-backed debt financing disbursed by the Brazilian National Development Bank and supporting policies to encourage delivery of strategic infrastructure.

We should take a leaf out of Brazil's book in our drive to become a world leader in offshore renewables. We should replace the cumbersome Renewables Obligation with a clear, simple and predictable feed-in tariff and introduce a new Green Investment Bank to encourage more low-cost capital into the renewable energy sector. The government should also work with the National Grid to support the construction of an offshore grid in the North Sea and with private investors to stimulate the redevelopment of ports so that turbine manufacturers and other companies supplying the offshore renewables industry base their operations in the UK. Targeted subsidies will be needed, but, in general, government support should be limited to infrastructure that supports a whole industry rather than any particular player within it.

Low-carbon living

One of the biggest sources of carbon emissions is transport, which remains almost completely reliant on expensive, volatile and polluting fuel derived from oil. As almost all oil is imported, transport's reliance on it is also bad for Britain's energy security. More than 75 per cent of the remaining proven oil reserves in the world is located in just three regions, where political instability or geopolitical ambition are prevalent: Africa, the former Soviet Union and the Persian Gulf. Outside these areas, oil production is migrating to frontiers such as the deep-water Gulf of Mexico and Canada's tar sands, where the environmental risks are becoming increasingly difficult to bear.

Sustainable biofuels offer one way to wean the transport sector off oil and to cut carbon emissions. Although there are bad biofuels, which cause deforestation (and should be banned), there are also many good biofuels, which should be encouraged. One of them is bioethanol made from sugarcane, which produces only a quarter the CO_2 of petrol and does not displace carbon-consuming trees. Another way of breaking the link between transport and the consumption of oil would be to deploy electric vehicles much more widely. The coalition should also be proactive here, working with the private sector and grid companies to build new infrastructure such as a network of vehicle charging points.

Increased electrification of transport will, of course, require the generation of more power. But we can offset any increased demand for electricity by helping people improve the energy efficiency of their homes. The key to achieving energy efficiency savings will be government orchestration of privately supplied financing structures that allow consumers to take out long-term loans for upfront investments in improved insulation or new boilers. These loans would be repaid over time via charges on consumers' utility bills. What is critical is that the amount repaid each month should be less than the value of the savings so that people feel an immediate benefit. In parallel, increasingly stringent efficiency standards should be applied to new houses and appliances. Combining these measures with a national roll-out of smart meters would help people cut their energy consumption by giving them the power to manage it intelligently.

As well as helping people cut their consumption of energy, the government should encourage them to generate energy closer to home. Combined heat and power (CHP) units, burning biomass or gas, offer particular promise. Such units generate not just electricity but also heat, which instead of being wasted can be piped around a house, office, housing estate or district. Consumers should be rewarded for investing in CHP units through feed-in tariffs. At the same time, large utilities should be encouraged to build and improve local heating networks. The addition of smaller, more numerous and more distributed sources of power generation will also require 'smarter' electricity grids. The government should work with the National Grid and the private sector to make the UK a leader in the development of this critical infrastructure.

Carbon tax

The single most important measure that government could take to incentivise investment in low carbon energy production and energy efficiency would be to put a meaningful price on carbon. At present, the UK's primary mechanism for pricing carbon at present is the EU's Emissions Trading Scheme (EU ETS). Lurking behind the EU ETS are some sound principles: that it is better to base a carbon reduction mechanism around an overall cap, as this gives environmental certainty, and that trading mechanisms maximise efficiency, allowing the market to discover the cheapest ways to cut overall carbon emissions. But the EU ETS has not worked in practice. The pricing signal it has generated has been too weak and too volatile to make a serious impact on investment decisions. The decision to allocate permits through a combination of auctions and 'free allocations' – where permits are given to polluters without charge – has created a playground for vested interests. The first phase of EU ETS ended up with the absurdity of large coal-fired generators making an overall profit from carbon trading. Meanwhile, the various nuances and quirks of EU ETS take years to understand, and enrich only lawyers and consultants.

The time has come for Britain to introduce a carbon tax and encourage other EU countries to do the same. Since it will be politically and practically difficult to phase out the EU ETS, such a tax should start off as a floor under the carbon price generated by the EU ETS. A carbon tax would thus apply initially to all plants covered by the EU ETS, with no loopholes for special interests. Over time, its coverage could be expanded to other sectors of the economy such as transport and agriculture. A carbon tax would send a clear, stable and simple price signal, improving the incentive to invest in energy efficiency, renewables and nuclear energy. A carbon tax also makes sense from the perspective of broader UK tax policy. Fundamentally, it makes sense to shift the burden of taxation onto pollutants, which society wants less of, and away from jobs and capital, which society wants more of. A carbon tax set at £20 per tonne would raise approximately £5 billion a year in new tax revenues immediately. These funds should be used to cut corporate taxes so that the overall tax burden on business is not increased. As the carbon tax is ramped up over time, and widens its coverage, it could become a major source of public revenues and facilitate substantial cuts in other forms of taxation that act as a brake on economic growth.

Multilateral negotiations

A harder-headed approach is also needed in international climate and energy policy. Focusing all of our diplomatic efforts on securing a legally binding global treaty has been a mistake, driven by Labour's misplaced faith in top-down solutions to every problem. The fact is that no political issue has yet proved powerful enough to galvanise truly global action and climate change is unlikely to be the first. The various UN summits have tended to reveal far more conflict than harmony, as the international community is forced to confront emotive disputes about how the burden for combating climate change should be shared between developed countries, who have been the source of most emissions to date and have enjoyed the associated economic growth, and developing countries, who will be source of most emissions in the future and will not tolerate being denied their turn at the economic trough.

The coalition government should focus on building agreement from the bottom up: national action and bilateral programmes flowing up into international agreements over time rather than the other way around. While grand cacophonies like the Copenhagen summit have been grabbing the headlines with scenes of diplomatic dysfunction on an epic scale, hundreds of national policies have been quietly enacted over the past decade or so. These policies are beginning to have a significant impact on the global energy mix. Some estimate that existing national policies alone could contribute two thirds of the carbon dioxide reductions needed to place the world on the road to low-carbon living. These national policies have in most cases been enacted despite, not because of, the Kyoto and Copenhagen summits.

International climate diplomacy would make much more impact if it concentrated on linking together national schemes into regional blocs and stitching together bilateral initiatives. In time, an international treaty could emerge, much as the World Trade Organization evolved from a web of regional and bilateral trade deals signed over the previous sixty years.

Britain should focus her limited diplomatic resources on a few targeted initiatives. We should divert some of our growing aid budget to support major funding deals to preserve tropical forests in Brazil and Indonesia, as deforestation is responsible for around 20 per cent of global greenhouse gas emissions. We should construct an equally bold and targeted initiative to support adaptation measures in a developing country that is particularly vulnerable to the impact of climate change, such as Bangladesh.

Removing fossil fuel subsidies should be another priority for British diplomats so that we can create a really level playing field for low-carbon energy sources. In a recent report, the International Energy Agency estimated that the world spent more than $500 billion subsidising fossil fuels in 2008, while less than a tenth of this amount was spent on subsidising renewables. Here we can collaborate closely with the US administration, as President Obama has made the elimination of fossil fuel subsidies one of his administration's major energy priorities. The British government should also work to remove barriers to the emerging global trade in renewable energy and the associated equipment, such as import tariffs against low-cost, environmentally sustainable biofuels from Brazil and some countries' local content requirements for renewable energy equipment.

Climate and energy policy is one area where the coalition should urge the EU to become more assertive and expand its role.

Russia's decision to cut off gas supplies to Ukraine in 2006 and again in 2009 demonstrated that energy security threats apply to Europe as a whole. If each of us negotiates our own supply agreements separately and in competition with each other, Russia will have the whip hand. If all the members of the EU get together and negotiate as a single customer, it is Russia that will be over a barrel. For the same reason, it is strongly in Britain's interest for the EU to promote the diversification of gas supplies through enhanced LNG infrastructure and to encourage unconventional gas exploration and new gas pipelines. Meanwhile, the EU's efforts to liberalise European energy markets and unbundle power generation from transmission and distribution would also enhance Britain's energy security and provide investment opportunities for UK businesses.

Less talk, more action

Politicians deal in words. Governments should deal in action. The tragedy of Britain's wasted decade is that hundreds of well-meaning people delivered millions of warm words about the looming threat of climate change but ministers did very little to change the way people live and businesses operate. The coalition needs to do the precise opposite. It should eschew sentiment, rhetoric and hyperbole and adopt Winston Churchill's governing motto, Action This Day. Ministers should spend less time sounding off at think tank seminars and international conferences and more time crunching the detail of feed-in tariffs, emissions standards, nuclear waste reprocessing plans and the capitalisation of the Green Investment Bank. It shouldn't be glamorous. It shouldn't make too many headlines. No babies will be kissed. But nothing the coalition government does will have more impact on the lives of our children and the generations who succeed them.

7. Boxing clever to keep Britain safe

If we look back at the Cold War, the remarkable thing about it is the speed with which it began to make sense. There is a danger, of course, in using hindsight to detect an order in events that seemed messy at the time. Still, it remains striking how quickly the conflict's patterns and institutions settled into a recognisable, even predictable, shape. Within five years of the end of the Second World War, NATO and the Warsaw Pact were in place, as were the Marshall plan, the Bretton Woods system and the United Nations. Europe had been reshaped at Yalta. Harry Truman's containment doctrine had been declared and would guide American statecraft for decades. The deterrent principle, which lent a kind of perverse stability to the 'war', was established when the Soviets acquired a bomb of their own. Berlin had emerged as the faultline of the conflict with Stalin's blockade of the city in 1948. In just a few years, most of the doctrines and organisations that would rule the second half of the twentieth century had been put in place.

Nothing like this great sorting out of the world has happened since 9/11, or in the two decades since the fall of the Berlin Wall. In his address to the Labour Party conference a few weeks after the Twin Towers fell, Tony Blair spoke vividly of a kaleidoscope being shaken: 'The pieces are in flux.' They still are.

America did not use its moment of solitary supremacy to design successor institutions; it left behind no new structures or conventions. For their part, Europeans, who had assumed that the end of the Cold War would shepherd in an international bureaucratic utopia of rule by summit and UN resolution, have been mugged by reality – or, more to the point, by the BRICs (Brazil, Russia, India and China). Emerging powers see the temples of multilateralism – the World Trade Organization, the International Monetary Fund, the G20 – as antiquated Western clubs bent on delaying their ascent to the top table. Vague bromides about 'global solutions to global problems', often aimed at supposedly inward-looking Conservatives by assorted Milibands, dodge the reality that international agreement on climate change, nuclear proliferation and trade has become more, not less, elusive. Meanwhile, the Cold War's martial successor, the war on terror, has dealt al-Qaeda crushing defeats but still lacks its own formal alliances, or commonly agreed-upon rules of engagement, or even much of a public profile. So much so that many ordinary people are barely conscious of the war going on, and some of their leaders are reluctant to even call it by that name.

But if the world lacks a shape, it very much has a direction. It has become so commonplace to observe the great shift in power from West to East that people often downplay its implications. The stark numbers chronicling economic growth in Asia are chastening enough; the military build-up it is likely to pay for in the longer run could be truly frightening. However, the most underrated challenge posed by a stirring Asia is ideological. The West can no longer argue credibly that economic development depends on political freedom, or even on particularly open and transparent markets. The Chinese model may, if pushed too heavy-handedly, jar with developing nations as much as the American one did. But countries charting a course to prosperity now know that a statist and authoritarian path is open to them. This may do more to undermine the appeal of the West than even the financial crisis. Nothing threatens a brand like a serious competitor.

So, in a world that is both stubbornly formless and tilting east, how should Britain make its way?

Labour's approach was restless idealism. The last government confounded preachers of British decline by putting the country at the vanguard of various struggles – against international terror, against dictators, against ethnic violence, against climate change, against global poverty. Many Conservatives, like me, admired the moral ambition of all this, as well as Labour's willingness to think globally even while talking of Britain's supposedly European destiny. Blair's government was, in many ways, like a mid-nineteenth-century Tory administration, with Blair playing the gun-boat diplomat while Brown signed the cheques to redeem the world's poor.

It made for a rousing vision in the years of plenty, but this missionary zeal is not a plausible strategy for the future. Hyperactivity costs money that Britain no longer has. It also claims lives, something that the British people are bearing with waning patience. Another Iraq or Afghanistan can never be totally ruled out. Blair arrived in power saying that his generation might turn out to be the first never to fight a war and ended up waging five. Iran's nuclear ambitions, or a Balkan relapse into ethnic feuding, could conceivably provoke a sixth. But a determination to slay dragons cannot be the organising principle behind our foreign policy plans in the next ten years.

Labour's internationalism also too often put values ahead of interests. The left may scoff at the idea that the original promise of an 'ethical dimension' in foreign policy ended up with the invasion of Iraq, but the last government was guilty of living up to that pledge too much, not too little. While foreign aid shot up, arms sales were tightened and 'environmental internationalism' became one of Britain's major priorities in global summitry, the national interest was sometimes neglected – or redefined to include almost anything.

It is remarkable that Britain remains the only country to have implemented all of its obligations under the Statute of Rome, which gave rise to the International Criminal Court in 1998. In and of itself, there is not much wrong with this. But it speaks to the left's slightly self-righteous certainty that, by playing the good guy, our 'soft' power is enhanced and more recalcitrant nations will eventually be shamed into following our example. It is not clear that the world works like that, or ever has done.

If Labour's expansive idealism is no longer right for Britain, neither is the apologetic retreat advocated in some quarters. There has always been a constituency of respectable opinion arguing that punching above our weight is more trouble than it is worth. Newspaper columnists such as Simon Jenkins and Matthew Parris, hardly voices of the pacifist left, lament the human and economic costs of Britain's global pretensions. The historian Correlli Barnett attributes our low productivity and inadequate infrastructure to our wasteful ambitions abroad, arguing that, while much of the rest of Europe turned inward after the war, investing their Marshall funds at home, we spent much of ours on preserving what was left of our global role. The debate over Trident has highlighted how widespread these attitudes remain in Westminster itself. Some Liberal Democrats, much of the Labour left and even former Tory

Defence Secretary Michael Portillo want Britain to give up its nuclear deterrent, which they see as an expensive narcotic feeding the national delusion that we remain a major player.

After the heart-rending losses we have endured in Iraq and Afghanistan, the voices urging retreat sense their moment. If continental Europe opted for a kind of geopolitical retirement after the Second World War, they ask, why not Britain? But they are wrong. Britain's decline is nothing like as vertiginous as often imagined; its 'weight' not so light as the pessimists would have it. Of course, there will eventually be an oligopoly of countries we cannot hope to match for sheer clout: America, China, India, Brazil. But our spot in the next tier of powers is safe, as long as we remain committed to it.

We are one of only two nations in the EU able to project military might beyond our shores and can certainly remain one of the top ten military powers for decades to come. We are the sixth-largest economy in the world, the fourth-largest destination of foreign investment, the second-largest holder of overseas investments. There is something surreal, not to mention sad, about a country with simultaneous membership of the EU, NATO, the UN Security Council's permanent five, the Commonwealth, the G8, the G20 and the nuclear club contemplating some kind of withdrawal from world affairs. For all the talk of imperial over-hang, our world-weary elites are guiltier of delusions of impotence than delusions of grandeur.

If not the vision espoused by Blair and Brown, or the gloomy alternative their most embittered critics would have us adopt, then what? Somewhere between quiet retreat and idealistic advance, there is energetic promotion of our national interest. Britain should be assertive and ambitious abroad, but for its own interests.

Saying so should not be noteworthy, but it is. David Cameron and William Hague would not be promising a clear-eyed focus on the national interest if people thought that Labour had provided enough of that over the past thirteen years.

Merely choosing *realpolitik* over *moralpolitik* in the abstract is one thing; defining what it means in policy terms is the bigger burden. Attempts to prescribe foreign policy often make the mistake of offering a view on everything. Magisterial *tours d'horizon* have their place, but pragmatism is about picking your fights and targeting your resources. Perhaps only America can justify a full-spectrum foreign policy. Second-rank powers have to set priorities.

Diplomacy

We are leaving an epoch in which the global high school was dominated by a brash but benign head boy who kept order on the playground through example, charisma and the occasional well-aimed kick (he doubles up as the star striker in the school's football team.) During these years, it made sense for Britain to be his long-suffering lieutenant. Not only did it give us influence over him, but family ties demanded it – our parents are related to his parents so we are cousins. The price was serving as a lightning rod for those aggrieved by his power and arrogance, but too nervous to say so to his face.

Increasingly, however, our cousin, the head boy, is becoming preoccupied with an awkward and unpredictable rival from the other side of town. This challenger avoids direct confrontations but is building his own power base by forming alliances of convenience with assorted malcontents, themselves gaining in strength compared to the decadent rich kids that the head boy has counted on in the past. The town may well be big enough for the both of them; but finding out will be uncomfortable for everyone living there.

In this time of flux, our role as sidekick will no longer be enough to guarantee our security, let alone the active promotion of our national interests. If the growing competition between the US and China becomes the dominating story of international politics, Britain must be nimble, resourceful and promiscuous, cementing its position as America's indispensable ally but pursuing its own interests in relation to China and developing independent alliances with India, Brazil and other rising powers.

Indeed, although our relationship with America is the most analysed of all our bilateral ties, it is also the most soporifically stable. The Atlantic alliance cannot be much closer than it was under Blair and Bush, or under Thatcher and Reagan; and it is unlikely to ever be much cooler than at the turn of the 1990s, when the elder Bush turned to Germany as his main European partner. These are reassuringly narrow limits for fluctuations in a diplomatic relationship. Our relationship with America will always be our most important; obsessing over exactly how 'special' it is at any given time seems futile.

The real diplomatic gains are to be made by cultivating the non-Western powers whose rise is the story of the early twenty-first century. The FCO's small budget is likely to be squeezed further so it should concentrate its resources on building ties with the BICs (Russia, struggling with demographic and other challenges, is not emerging quite as spectacularly as Brazil, India and China) and the next tier of emerging powers. It no longer makes sense for the most able and experienced of our diplomatic corps to end up in the capitals of long-standing allies. Washington, Paris and Berlin may be wonderful places to age gracefully, but there is little value to be added there. The new destinations for the FCO's brightest and best should not only be Beijing, Delhi and Brasilia, but also the likes of Ankara, Seoul and Jakarta.

Underpinning this reallocation of diplomatic resources should be a strategy. In every region of the globe, Britain should decide upon a few pivotal relationships, and identify one or two concrete ways in which it can earn influence over those countries. In the Near and Middle East, Britain's obvious options are Turkey and Israel; it can serve both of them as their biggest champions in Europe, a place where they struggle for a fair hearing. Many politicians and voters in both countries aspire to EU membership. Britain should support their claims (though with tight restrictions on the freedom of the seventy million Turks and seven million Israelis to work anywhere in Europe). Crucially, it should also push the idea of making each country's accession dependent on the other's. This would immediately give them a strategic interest in the other's development, as well as in convivial relations between them. The EU rightly boasts of its ability to lure countries into liberal and pacific patterns of behaviour by offering them the prize of membership, but this is a reason to extend it to those countries that would benefit the most from such influence, not to draw a spurious line between 'real' Europe (which looks rather like the old Christendom) and the 'other'.

In Asia, countries such as Malaysia and Indonesia stand to benefit from the help of outside expertise in counter-terror intelligence and military counter-insurgency. Britain has acquired plenty of both from its experiences at home and abroad. With regard to Latin America, Britain should be vociferous in arguing that Brazil deserves permanent membership of the Security Council and should work with the emerging colossus on the protection of the rainforest (of which more below) and the development of international trade in bioethanol.

It is harder for Britain to make itself indispensable to the nascent giants of Asia. Our approach to China can differ little from that of most European nations. Unless vital interests are stake, we should stay out of any diplomatic showdowns that break out between Beijing and Washington in the coming years. After all, we are powerless to influence the issues they are likely to struggle over, which essentially boil down to mastery of east Asia. Pragmatism is about knowing when you don't have a dog in a fight.

With a heavy heart, we are also coming to understand the futility of anything more than perfunctory pressuring of China on human rights and democratic reform. Its internal politics are changing and will continue to change, but at a barely perceptible crawl. Loud lobbying from outside will only make it easier for reactionaries to slander political reform as a Western plot to undermine Chinese stability. At both the European and national level, our engagement with China for the foreseeable future will take the form of economic diplomacy to secure access to its vast markets. Even much smaller countries than Britain will have broader foreign policies towards China, either because of geographical proximity, like Malaysia, or because they control resources craved by the Chinese, like Australia. That is as it should be. Nostalgia for our time as serious players in east Asia should not deflect us from our narrow, hard-headed focus on trade and investment with China.

British–Indian relations, however, have the potential to be richer, so it was exactly the right destination for David Cameron to lead his first all-singing, all-dancing delegation as Prime Minister. Our efforts to enlist Pakistan in the fight against al-Qaeda internationally and the Taleban in Helmand have sometimes risked nudging us away from our more obvious and important ally in the region. David Miliband's visit to India after the 2008 terrorist attacks in Mumbai went down worse than many in Westminster realise; his attempts at a nuanced, pseudo-academic analysis of Islamist terrorism was not what his traumatised hosts were expecting.

The coalition government has clearly understood that it cannot rely on the passage of time to undo the damage. The Prime Minister's strong words about Pakistan were designed to draw a line and show that the new government in Britain will never muddy its clear line in support of a democracy that is on the front line of the global war against terror. William Hague should now consider reshaping the ministerial portfolios in the FCO so that there is a dedicated minister or under-secretary for the subcontinent, or perhaps a special envoy to India. Whatever the title of the post, a strong signal would be sent if the first appointment were someone with a defence or counter-terror background. Experience should also be a criterion; the cult of youth that allows thirty- and forty-somethings to run governments, companies and newspapers in Britain is not always shared abroad, especially in Asia. Lord Robertson of Port Ellen, the former Defence Secretary and NATO secretary general, would be a suitable candidate for the role. We should also allow British entrepreneurs and industrialists to shape our economic diplomacy with India. They are in a better position than any civil servant to know which barriers to trade are most onerous, which sectors are most promising, and which skills Britain lacks that India has in abundance (and vice versa).

Again, none of this should be guided by a soft-headed sense of internationalism. We have a profound strategic interest in close relations with this emerging colossus. To end up with anything less – given the bonds forged with India through history, the English language and the many Indians who have made Britain their home – would be a remarkable failure.

There should be one exception to this focus of our diplomatic energies on the rising powers of Asia and Latin America, one major Western power centre which merits a ruthless focus from the British government – Brussels.

The European Union

One of the casualties of the past thirteen years is the notion that British Euroscepticism is a flimsy thing that could be blown away if only politicians would make the case for the EU. Under their most explicitly pro-European government ever, the British actually grew more hostile to the Union. And that was before the euro crisis. If some kind of fiscal co-ordination emerges in the euro zone to bolster the single currency, the prospect of Britain ever joining would plunge from unlikely to unimaginable.

Blair represented the final, failed effort to turn Britain into a truly European nation, but the alternative is not an equally ideological flirtation with withdrawal from the EU. What is needed is remorselessly self-interested participation. In Brussels, Britain should expend precious political capital on the defensive fight to retain powers for itself, and win back some which were given up in the past. It should not waste it on broad and fanciful projects to remake the EU along British lines.

The Blairite mission to liberalise Europe by putting Britain at its 'heart' was a failure. Britain has championed the Lisbon agenda of economic reforms since they were drawn up over a decade ago, but to little avail. If anything persuades continental economies to loosen their labour markets and trim their public-sector pensions, it will be the dawning recognition that the European social model cannot pay for itself. Similarly, years of British lobbying to reform the Common Agricultural Policy produced the feeblest of deals, with Britain giving up a large chunk of its rebate in return for a nebulous commitment to examine the farm subsidy regime.

Our basic diplomatic rule in Brussels must be to spare Britain from integration, not to try and shape the nature of that integration. For example, we should aim to secure opt-outs from any new EU law that threatens our competitiveness, rather than haggle for a slightly less draconian version of the law. More broadly, we should welcome the prospect of a 'core' and 'periphery' EU. Britain once feared this 'variable geometry', at times out of Blairite determination to be at Europe's heart, at other times because of the Foreign Office's habitual fear that we would end up eventually joining institutions that we were not there to shape from the start. Over time, though, Europe *à la carte* has effectively become the British vision, without anyone ever expounding it in a Bruges-style speech. Perhaps the time for such a statement has come. This model of Europe has the added virtues of reflecting existing realities – what is the euro zone if not the core of the EU? – and of commanding the support of another big member state, France.

Indeed, France is in many ways the model Britain should emulate. The British discourse lazily invokes the 'Franco-German axis' as if both countries are indistinguishably *communautaire*. In truth, France sees Europe as a way of advancing national interests; Germany, with its traumatic experience of the nation-state, views it more loftily as an opportunity to transcend them (though even this shows some signs of fading). Examples of French intransigence abound: the epic delays in 'transposing' directives into national law; the flouting of the euro zone's stability and growth pact almost as soon as it was inaugurated; the 21-year defiance of the EU's fisheries policy; the insistence on the European Parliament dividing its time between Brussels and Strasbourg. France is willing to be distinctly un-European whenever it suits its interests. So should Britain.

There are some integrationist projects in the EU that would serve collective interests as well as our own, but which will probably be difficult to achieve. Britain should signal its support for these, but not invest much diplomatic capital on their active promotion. Defence co-operation, for example, has the potential to give Europe a louder voice abroad while reducing the costly duplication of military assets across different countries, most particularly Britain and France. Principled hostility to the idea has also faded. America is now relaxed about the Europeans getting their military house in order, and any threat to NATO has disappeared since France's re-entry into its command structure.

Another example is greater European co-ordination of energy policy. Russia has had a disturbingly easy time peeling some EU countries, most obviously Germany, away from the rest when it comes to negotiating supply deals for oil and gas. Europe's inability to speak with one voice on world affairs is a natural reflection of different histories and cultures; its struggle to achieve coherence on something as vital as its own energy supplies is sheer stupidity. But, while clear about the goal, we should not waste too much diplomatic capital on a mission to unify twenty-seven different national energy policies, and let the Commission take the lead.

If Britain is to champion a cause beyond the issue-by-issue defence of its own tightly defined interests, it is enlargement. A wider EU is a looser one. Enlargement is regarded increasingly warily by federalists for exactly that reason. They have brandished the euro crisis as proof of the chaos that comes with having too diverse a club. Britain should challenge this logic and, while insisting on tight restrictions on the freedom to work anywhere in the EU that Labour foolishly waived when Poland and other eastern European countries joined, we should brand ourselves as the unambiguous friends of the aspirant members. We should lobby on behalf of the official candidate countries (Turkey, Macedonia and Croatia, which will join next year) as well as those nations further back in the accession process, including Albania, Serbia and Bosnia & Herzegovina, and longer-term contenders such as Israel. We should also fight the gradual tightening of the conditions for accession, something which delayed Croatia's entry and is designed to make Turkey's virtually impossible.

Security

The war in Afghanistan was absolutely unavoidable; it is impossible to conceive of a credible response to 9/11 that left al-Qaeda's base of operations untouched. The war in Iraq was a war we chose but, ultimately, it was the right choice. Despite being abominably executed for much of the 3½ years between the toppling of Saddam and the surge of 2006, it is increasingly hard to describe the creation of a pluralist society and broadly pro-Western democracy, sandwiched between Syria, Saudi Arabia and Iran, as a mistake.

But Britain must now design a military posture for the world after Iraq and Afghanistan. Although the government insists that the review will be informed by real-world threats and interests, and not by the dearth of funds available, spending cuts are inevitable. There was a funding shortfall even before the fiscal crisis. What should go? The British orthodoxy in defence has been to maintain a little bit of everything: a sizeable army, a deep-strike air force, a blue-water navy, a nuclear deterrent and some of the world's premier special forces. The crude choice is between more or less giving up on at least one of these or continuing to salami-slice across all the services.

The less risky of these two hazardous options is the second. Phasing out the Royal Air Force or reducing our navy to a territorial defence fleet would make us reliant on allies if we were to fight a distant war. That makes sense for an American-led mission such as Iraq or Afghanistan, but what if the interests at stake are exclusively British? It was hard enough to obtain American help of any kind in the Falklands War of 1982; we could not count on them for aircraft carriers and fighter jets if another crisis broke out there. Nor can we predict the nature of the threats this country will face in the future. A decade ago, when the conflicts of the day were short, sharp, humanitarian interventions like those in Kosovo and Sierra Leone, some experts were certain that this would be the new way of war. Prolonged deployments of massed land armies seemed unimaginable: the future lay in air power and small, mobile units. A few years later, we were in Iraq and Afghanistan. The lesson is unavoidable: we must have all military options available to us, even if only in diminished form.

Our nuclear deterrent is, rightly, out of bounds in the defence review. To argue for nuclear disarmament, or indeed any radical military shrinkage, is to argue for geopolitical retreat. Military power is what converts economic power into political power. Japan is a vast economy, exporter and net creditor but, with only defensive forces, as mandated by its constitution, 'What does Tokyo think?' is not the feverish diplomatic question it should be. Something similar is true of Germany, at least outside of its EU comfort zone. At the other extreme is Russia. Even during its mid-1990s nadir, or in its current struggles with grim demographics and depleted foreign reserves, it never stopped mattering. The magnitude of its military hardware has seen to that.

The government should also be rigorous in how it defines security. Labour talked modishly of climate change, mass migration flows, pandemics and the like as issues of national security. And though the principle of co-ordinating the various policy areas relating to security is sound, the new National Security Council could end up including almost anything within its remit if it does not adhere to a tight, codified definition of what counts as security. A recent Chatham House report proposes a definition that includes '*direct threats* to British citizens that could have *severe consequences* for their welfare, within *a limited horizon* (say 5–10 years)' (emphasis in original). This, say the authors, would mean that terrorism, organised crime, natural disasters and cyber-attacks on key infrastructure should be treated as national security threats, whereas climate change, resource scarcity and global economic problems should not. Too expansive a definition of security risks diluting our focus on the most basic, mortal threats facing our country.

International aid

After defence, the most expensive item of Britain's international work is aid. £6.3 billion was spent on it in 2008; this may have to rise to something in the region of £12 billion in order to meet the government's target of devoting 0.7 per cent of GDP to international development by 2013. In an age of austerity, with cuts being made to armed forces that have paid a heavy blood price for British security for much of the past decade, it would not be heartless to abandon the 0.7 per cent target. The temptation should be resisted, however. At what is still a relatively small cost, aid makes a tangible difference in the developing world, perhaps averting the need for more costly Western interventions later. After years of exhorting the rest of the rich world to follow its generous example, Britain's reputation and credibility would suffer if it ditched the spending target. But the taxpayer is entitled to expect our aid operation to do something for British interests in return.

The coalition should push to the limit the OECD's restrictions on what counts as aid, and expand the contribution from the aid budget to reconstruction and development projects run by the military and the diplomatic service in Afghanistan and Iraq. Currently, 12 per cent of our total aid budget is spent by other departments than DfID; this should double by 2013.

The government should also adopt four new priorities for aid spending, and devote the bulk of future increases in the aid budget to them. The first should be support for tropical countries' efforts to combat deforestation and prepare for the possibility of climate change. The creation of long-running programmes to invest in local efforts to protect the rainforest in Brazil and Indonesia would support our diplomatic focus on these newly crucial powers. It would also show that we have the humility to acknowledge our responsibility, as one of the countries whose early industrialisation made a big contribution to the accumulation of greenhouse gases, to help newly industrialising countries find a different, and less damaging, path for economic development. We should also invest a good chunk of aid in helping countries such as Bangladesh find ways to adapt to the possibility of rising sea levels.

The second new priority for foreign aid should be to support the stabilisation of countries that are major actual or potential sources of illegal immigrants to Britain. It will be much easier to win public support for growth in the aid budget, at a time of tax rises and expenditure cuts, if the British people feel that it is helping reduce the pressure on their local public services.

The third new priority should be to make it easy and affordable for people across the developing world to learn the Queen's English – or, at the very least, Stephen Fry's. The BBC World Service runs a good online service with resources for teachers, journalists and businesspeople. More money should be invested in initiatives like this, as well as in efforts by the British Council and others to provide materials and teaching support to local schools and colleges on the ground. Helping people learn English not only expands their opportunities but also makes it more likely that they will visit Britain, buy from Britain, and invest in Britain in years to come.

The fourth new priority should be the endowment of a generous scholarship programme, bringing several hundred of the brightest graduates from China, India, Brazil and other rising powers to Britain's finest universities for 1–2 years' study. When, in 1902, Cecil Rhodes left money to set up the Rhodes Scholarships in his will, he did so because he thought that 'a good understanding between England, Germany and the United States of America will secure the peace of the world'. Nothing would do more to cement the importance of Britain in the minds of the new elites of Asia and Latin America, or to create lasting networks of friendly relations between their countries and our own, than for the best among them to have spent a year or two studying at Oxford, Cambridge or the LSE.

Much of this will enrage the purists of the aid community. But it is neither defensible nor politically viable for Britain to spend 0.7 per cent of its national income on aid during a fiscal crisis without demanding something in return. The aid lobby should remember the most likely alternative to this new realism: that taxpayers, who never supported the rapid expansion of foreign aid after 1997, lose patience entirely and demand a more dramatic pruning of Britain's good works abroad.

Back to the future

In adopting a more independent, pragmatic and free-wheeling approach to international affairs, Britain will be returning to the attitudes that defined our rise to greatness in the seventeenth and eighteenth centuries. Acting as sidekick to the America's head boy was the right course in the latter half of the twentieth century, because this was the only way to defend our values and our interests in the face of the totalitarian threat. But it required a level of subservience that even the most instinctive pro-American like me couldn't help but find irksome. As the world moves into an era of multi-dimensional competition between many powers, old and new, East and West, North and South, Britain can renew the strategy that made this collection of islands the world's greatest trading nation. We should be aggressive in the promotion of our national interest, suspicious of entanglements and permanent alliances, cautious about picking fights we cannot win, and implacable in defence of our freedom.

Conclusion

Britain faces mammoth challenges. The changes that the new government will have to make will have a seismic impact on how people live their lives and how communities work. Implementing them will cause dislocation and suffering to many people. Public patience will be stretched close to breaking point and this will place enormous pressure on MPs, who will bear the brunt of people's fury as services and benefits are cut, while taxes and charges go up.

The coalition government has innate strengths – and obvious vulnerabilities. It commands a large majority in the House of Commons, which should withstand rebellions on all but the most existential issues. It can speak to the British people, knowing that 60 per cent of them voted for one or other of the parties and backed the leadership of either David Cameron or Nick Clegg. But it cannot assume the instinctive discipline that comes from a shared history or membership of the same club. As the missiles rain down, Conservatives and Liberal Democrats will stick together only if each party's MPs believe that they are being true to their most fundamental values and are making steady progress on the issues that matter most to them.

In this book, I have tried to sketch out a programme of

government that would, over ten years, deliver a fairer, stronger, freer country, and a society in which people are more responsible, more trusting and more at ease with their neighbours and their compatriots. These are goals that inspire Conservatives and Liberal Democrats in equal measure. I have also tried to suggest methods of reform that sit comfortably with our shared values: communities, competition and choice; incentives, innovation and independence. It is by handing power to the men and women of Britain and respecting the autonomy of free institutions that this government will achieve the changes it seeks.

But a shared sense of direction, of being engaged in a worthwhile mission, will not be sufficient to keep the two parties united. We politicians are not saints (I need hardly point out) – and we are not devoid of vanity or ambition. Conservative and Liberal Democrat MPs need to feel that we are more likely to win re-election, both individually and as a government, if we support the coalition, than if we turn our backs on it. Because of this, and because I believe that a liberal conservative government is Britain's best hope of surmounting the challenges that lie ahead, I want to conclude this book by urging David Cameron and Nick Clegg to announce this autumn that they want their parties to agree to an electoral pact for the general election due on 7 May 2015.

The pact would be in two parts, to deal with each of the possible outcomes to the referendum on the Alternative Vote that is to be held in May 2011. If the British people choose to keep the First Past the Post electoral system of electing MPs, as I hope, the pact would give Conservative parliamentary candidates in Conservative-held constituencies a free run against other parties: the Liberal Democrats would not put up a candidate and would urge their supporters to vote Conservative. Liberal Democrat candidates in the seats they hold would be granted an equivalent free run by the Conservatives: we would not put up a candidate and would urge our supporters to vote Liberal Democrat. With all constituency boundaries likely to change as a result of the equalisation of constituency sizes and the reduction in the number of MPs, the calculation of which seats are held by which party will have to be done on the basis of the notional majorities that would have been achieved if the last election had been fought on the new boundaries. The two parties should also try and agree which of them should contest the most marginal Labour, Scottish Nationalist and Welsh Nationalist seats.

If the British people decide to embrace the Alternative Vote, the pact would require the Conservative Party (and all Conservative candidates) to urge their supporters to give their second-preference vote to the Liberal Democrats, and would require the Liberal Democrats (and all their candidates) to do likewise for the Conservatives.

It is important that the proposal for an electoral pact is put to both parties in the next few months and is agreed before the start of 2011 so that every one of both parties' MPs understands that flirting with losing the whip by voting against the government on key legislation might also entail losing the protection of the electoral pact and that this might make it much harder to win re-election in 2015.

Two of my political heroes, John F. Kennedy and Ronald Reagan, spoke of their country as 'a shining city upon a hill'. We lucky few who get to spend our lives on this island know that there is also something special about Britain, something that sets us apart from other nations. At its best, Britain can be an example to the world: we can lead the way and give others a glimpse of a better future. We did it when Magna Carta established the principle of habeas corpus and limited the power of kings. We did it when William Wilberforce led a long campaign to rid the world of the slave trade. We did it when, with Winston Churchill, Britain stood alone. Today we face different demons, less fearsome but still daunting. And the whole country is asking, 'How do we get out of this slough of despond?'

I believe we all know which way's up. The path lies before us, long and rocky, but at its end we can see the sunlit ramparts of that city on a hill. Destiny has asked Conservatives and Liberal Democrats to put down their swords and work together for the nation's good. It was a coalition under Conservative leadership that won the war against fascism; it will be a coalition under Conservative leadership that restores our pride, prosperity and peace.

Also available from Biteback

MAKING THE DIFFERENCE
Essays in honour of Shirley Williams

Published to celebrate the life and career of one of the most
influential women in British politics, *Making the Difference* is a
collection of essays by Baroness Williams's peers, contemporaries
and protégés on the themes and issues she has campaigned on
during the course of an inspirational career in politics spanning
five decades. The editor, Andrew Duff, has brought together
an impressive group of contributors for this important book,
demonstrating the esteem and affection felt for this
remarkable politician.

240pp Hardback, £19.99

Available from all good bookshops or order from
www.bitebackpublishing.com

Also available from Biteback

CAMPAIGN 2010
The Making of the Prime Minister
Nicholas Jones

The countdown to the coalition – as viewed by one of
Westminster's most seasoned observers.

In the run-up to the general election of May 2010 it was
universally acknowledged that whatever the outcome, this vote
would start a new chapter in British political history.

But none of the soap opera of the weeks leading up to 6 May
could match the drama of the days following the inconclusive
result. A fresh chapter in history – and a fresh level of political
theatre incisively described by Nicholas Jones.

400pp Paperback, £9.99

Available from all good bookshops or order from
www.bitebackpublishing.com

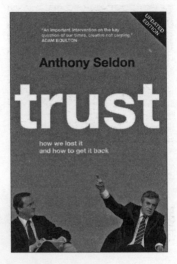

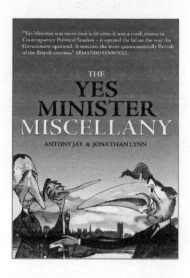